John Lee Hooker Guitar

Authentic Tablature Transcriptions Off the Original Recordings
Transcribed by Richard DeVinck

NEW ENLARGED EDITION!

CONTENTS

John Lee Hooker - Talks About the Early Years	8
Souvenir Photo Section	2
Performance Notes by Richard DeVinck	15
Transcriber's Biographical Notes	14
Selected Discography	15
The Tablature Notation	16

THE SONGS

Baby, How Can You Do It?	19
Boogie Chillen'	34
Cold Chills All Over Me	46
Crawlin' King Snake	145
Do My Baby Think Of Me?	168
Hello Baby (Don't You Remember Me?)	52
Hobo Blues	178
I Got The Key (Key To The Highway)	60
I'm Gonna Git Me A Woman	67
I'm In The Mood	74
It Hurts Me So	92
John L.'s House Rent Boogie	100
Let's Talk It Over	85
Queen Bee	112
Rock Me, Mama	119
Sally Mae	124
This is 19 And 52, Babe (Turn Over A New Leaf)	154
Weepin' Willow Boogie	132

©1992, 1994 LaCienega Music
All Rights Reserved

Cover photo by Bill Reitzel

Catalog No. 07-4034
Please write for Free catalog of Great Blues Guitar Books

Exclusive Distrubutor:
Creative Concepts Publishing Corporation, 410 Bryant Circle, Box 848, Ojai, CA 93024

JOHN LEE HOOKER (SECOND FROM RIGHT)

JOHN LEE HOOKER AND BONNIE RAITT

WITH BONNIE RAITT

JOHN LEE HOOKER AND ROBERT JUNIOR LOCKWOOD

WITH ROBERT CRAY

John Lee Hooker
Talks About the Early Years
Interviewed by Jim & Amy O'Neal
for Living Blues Magazine #44

Since you're the "King of the Boogie," maybe you can tell us something about how the boogie developed.

Well, I tell you, really how it started way back, I'm the first person that really got the boogie goin'. Everybody now is boogie-this and boogie-that – but I am the original. And the word come from *Boogie Chillen*. When *Boogie Chillen* first come out, everywhere you went you would hear that, 'cause that was a new beat to the blues then. That was the boogie. Then it laid dead for years and years and then I revived it. And brushed it up, and really kicked it off again with me and Canned Heat. Canned Heat was playing my style some anyway. Remember they did this number *On The Road Again*. That thing come out, it caught afire. From then on everybody else was boogie-this, boogie-that, boogie fever, and all this. They all had my beat. They all had taken it from the boogie. And so that's why they called me the originator of the boogie, which I am. So, anywhere I go, if I don't play that, the people, they're let down, you know. I love to play it, too, 'cause I gets off on it. But also I gets off on my older stuff too. Just sittin' down playing just the blues, then I get 'em to listenin'. And then before I come down I hit them with the boogie and then I get them all up in the air. But I get 'em all ready for it first with slow blues. Then on the last I'll hit 'em with the boogie and get 'em all really carried away. Honest the truth, I get carried away, too. 'Cause I feel it just as much as they do. People ask me how do I do it? I say, "It's just there. I can't explain it. It just comes out." And, "You're the only man I see at your age can hop around like a little spring chicken." I say, "Well, I well reserve my body, I mean I well reserve myself as much as I can. It may sound funny to you, I'm not old, I've just been here for a while." [Laughs.] I feel good and I do appreciate and honor the people that given me the name, the "King of the Boogie," which I think I deserve, because I originated it way back in '49 and then I brought it up to date. I'm gonna keep it goin', but it may be under just a little bit different thing but it's gonna be on the same order. I appreciate the people that doin' the boogie, you know, they're tryin' to do it. You know, when they do it, or do somethin' like me, that makes me much more famous and thought of, you see what I mean? "That's John Lee Hooker. They're doin' John Lee Hooker's thing." And I don't get up tight when I hear somebody, copyin' it or doin' it. But I like for 'em to give me credit for it. Some of 'em do and some of 'em don't.

Was there a way the boogie developed down South before you went to Detroit?

Well, down South I hadn't never thought of it, honest the truth. I was just a kid then. I developed that when I was in Detroit. But I did know about all this stuff. Down there they were callin' it the boogie woogie. They wasn't sayin' "boogie," they was sayin', "doin' the boogie woogie." And as the years went by, and I got up here and I come to Detroit – and when I did get a chance to get famous, I did this thing called *Boogie Chillen*. I didn't say boogie woogie – I said *Boogie Chillen*.

Were there any musicians you heard doing things similar to the boogie?

You mean when I was young? You mean what I'm doing now? No, this style I'm doin' now wasn't nothin' like way back there, you know. They wasn't even playin' this kind of music. Like I say, what they was doing then they was callin' the boogie woogie. It was just maybe a guitar, and a old piano, sit down playin' the boogie woogie. The barrelhouse, and stuff like that. It wasn't the type of music, the boogie, that they're doin' now with this tremendous beat and rhythm and disco beat and stuff like that. But it's the same music, but it's just come up to date and they changed it. The stuff they're doin' now – it's taken from the blues. The music they call soul music, you know, it's the blues. So disco is no soul; rock 'n roll is not soul. The *blues* is soul. And you know, I just can't get through a lot of people's heads, but any blues singer will tell you, soul music is the blues. 'Cause it come from the soul. From the heart and soul – you feels is. But this other stuff they're doin', what they call soul, they're just doin' it either to be seen or be heard, and this one tryin' to outdo the other one and tryin' to get a hit. But the blues is a thing just go along and along

continued from page 1

just like Old Man River. You feels it. Some people have lived it. I know I have.

What was it like when you started out down South?
Well, I never did have a hard time 'cause my dad had a big farm down there. But I know it was rough. I didn't experience it 'cause I left there when I was 14, 'cause I was playin' music when I was 12 or 14. I ran away from home. My dad came and got me. I ran off from my dad and I went to Memphis. I stayed around about two months. I was workin' at a movie picture show, the New Daisy, and then goin' to school when I could. And when I couldn't, I didn't go, you know. And my dad followed me. He come got me, I stayed about three months. Then I come to Detroit. And that's where I was raised up at.

Do you know where the word "boogie" came from? What it originally meant?
The word "boogie?" Well, the word "boogie"? Well, the word "boogie" come from years and years and years back – way before I was born. The boogie comes from the boogie woogie. "Let's boogie," you know. But that's been around ever since there's been a world. And then, you know, all that come from the blues and stuff like that, the old barrelhouse, piano boogie. There'd be a guy on a piano by hisself and there's someone sittin' up and drinkin' liquor and they're playing the boogie woogie. See, I got all them ideas, you know, and I really got famous. And see, I haves a lot of ideas, you know, about different things. And then I did 'em, you know.

When people think of boogie woogie, they think of piano players more.
Yeah. Right.

So did any of your style come from listening to the piano players?
No. My style come from my stepfather, Will Moore. The style I'm playing now, that's what he was playing. My style is my stepfather's style. See, I learned from him. He was a guitar player. The same thing I'm doin' now. I'm doin' it *identical* to his style. And nobody else plays that style. I got a style that nobody else has.

Where did it come from – where did he get it?
I don't know. I think him and another guy used to play together all the time: Charley Patton. Yeah, they would play together, just two guitars.

Did you ever see Charley Patton with your stepfather?
No, I didn't. They would play around the little honky-tonk joints and things. But I couldn't get out to those places, you know, 'cause I was too little. Man, I wanted to see that man so bad. Yeah, I used to play one of his old records, *Catch My Pony,* and *Saddle Up My Black Mare.* I used to hear my stepdaddy play that. Yeah, and I learned it from him. I know he did play around with Charley Patton, and Blind Blake, and people like that. I heard of those people, I never did see them. I heard their records – Leroy Carr, piano player. I heard all of them. My stepfather, he saw those people. I was influenced some by them. Blind Lemon – I never see him – one man, he was my idol, too – Blind Lemon Jefferson. That's B.B. King's idol, too.

Are you doing some of the same songs your step-father sang?
No. I'm not doin' none of his songs. I don't even know any of his songs. I just know his style on the guitar. He taught me the style. But the songs, I wrote them myself, and I had my own voice. I used to sing in church. I used to sing spirituals. I was with a spiritual group, and then when I came up they said, "Oh, but that kid – gotta go hear that kid sing!" When I'd get up in church, people just loved it – like they just started hollerin' and screamin' about the singin', you know. I had such a voice, and well, I still do, but I was still tryin' to play guitar then. I was playin' a little bit. I would just sing and play my guitar and my stepfather'd look at me and he'd say, "Where'd you get that voice from?!" Said, "I don't know." 'Cause it was just there, you know.

That was long before electric guitars.
Oh, long before. The first electric guitar I ever played was T-Bone Walker's. I thought I had a piece of gold in my hands when I had that thing!

When you were in Memphis, were you playing there?
No. Well, I was playing some, you know, but nobody know me. Me and B.B. and them, we just messed around there. But B.B. stayed there for a while. Me and B.B. and Bobby (Bland), we were playin' around Memphis, for house parties there. In West Memphis, you know, we went over there across the bridge. We'd go over there and party all night and mess around. And a lot of clubs, they wouldn't let me in – they usually wouldn't let us in 'cause we wasn't old enough. So we just played around at house parties and things, which we'd get just as big a kick out of – all we

continued from page 2

wanted was a drink of liquor – that's what we'd get, forget about the money.

Did you see any of the bands, like the bigger name people who were around there then?
Yeah, I saw some of 'em. Yeah, I saw this guy – one of the greatest things in the world – W.C. Handy. I used to go to the theater.

Weren't you in Cincinnati for a while?
Oh, yeah, I stayed there about three years. But I didn't get no break there and I left. I was in Cincinnati when I was around about 18, maybe somewhere like that. I wasn't doin' anything. I really didn't become known until I got in Detroit. You know, a lot of people admired me in these places where I would play at in these other cities, like Cincinnati, but I didn't get a break until I got into Detroit. There was a record company there [Cincinnati] called King Records, but they never did get to hear me [at that time]. I was just beginnin' to kind of get into it. I could play a little bit. I got more and more experience when I got into Cincinnati and Detroit, and playin' around them honky-tonk joints. Anywhere I could play, money or no money, you know. Sometimes I'd get thrown out of clubs 'cause I wasn't old enough. I'd put my age up and when they found out I was lyin', they'd kick me out.

When you went to Detroit, how did you get started playing? When you were just playin' around the city, in clubs?
Oh, I wasn't playin' any clubs. I was just playing around house parties and once in a while I'd go in a club and sit in, you know. I was workin' at a day job, then playin' house parties. When I came to Detroit, there was a little company called Sensation Records – a little old label. It no longer exists. Bernie Besman and Elmer Barber, this Jewish guy and this black cat. This black cat, he had that record store there in Detroit – him and Bernie was really good friends. Bernie Besman had this big, big distributor, it was downtown. And this guy, Barber, he come to a house party one night and heard me playing. That's when he invited me down to his place. He had a little studio in the back, he would cut tapes and blanks on different artists. He had some of every blues singer back there but he hadn't never been able to produce any of 'em on a major record company but me. When he heard me, he said it was the best he had ever heard. He said he'd never heard a style like this. See, a lot of 'em sounded most alike, he said, but I was so outstanding. He said, "I know somebody who would *love* to get a hold of you." I said, "Aw, man, people been tellin' me that for what – five or six years or 10 years and nobody gave me a break. They been givin' me all this baloney." And he said, "Yeah, no kidding?" He took me down to this big, huge place – all the records and these big executives settin' up in there, and then I went back in the office and Barber, he presented me to Bernie Besman. A tape, a dub, you know. They listened to it. They said, "Oh. Is this you?" I said, "Yeah." "Man, I tell you, you got somethin' different, ain't nobody else got. I never heard a voice like that. Do you want to record?" I said, "Yeah. But I've been jived so much, I don't know if y'all just putting me on. They said, "No, no, kid," he said. "We're not puttin' you on. You're really good. You've written them songs on there?" I said, "Yeah." And then him and Barber went back in the room and talked. I'm sittin' back in there, you know, I don't know that they was talkin' about. And after a while, Barber said, "I got good news." So I said, "What is it?" He said, "I can get you a recordin' contract." And he say, "You can record in a week's time. We can go in the studio." And I said, "Yeah?" He said, "You can get $1000 up front." I hadn't never had that much money. I said, "Huh?!" [Laughs.] I said, "Say that again." He said, "We'll give you $1000 up front and a cent and a half royalty." I said, "Yeah, I'll take it." So we went back and we got to work. Then we went in the studio that Wednesday – we recorded in about three weeks. They put out the 78's. They throwed that *Boogie Chillen* out and *Sally Mae* on the other side [on Modern Records]. The thing caught afire. It was ringin' all across the country. When it come out, every jukebox you went to, every place you went to, every drug store you went, everywhere you went – department stores, they were playin' it in there. I felt good, you know. And I was workin' in Detroit in a factory there for a while. Then I quit my job. I said, "No, I ain't workin' no more!" He said, "John, you got a good job." I said, "Yeah, but I don't want it. I got a hit record. I got to get on the road." Yeah, they laughed, you know.

Did you go on the road after that?
Yeah. They said, "Well, I wish you well. Yeah, 'cause I heard the record. It's playing everywhere. I was expectin' that outta you." I said, "Wouldn't you do it?" He said, "Yeah. Well, anytime you want to come back – well, I doubt it, but you can always come back." I said, "Thank you for your offer. Get my check ready." Ever since then, you know, hit after hit. I

continued from page 3

gotta get hit after hit. I stayed on the road all the time. Sometime we'd be gone about four and five months before we'd come home. *Boogie Chillen* become the natural-born No. 1 hit all over – it stayed No. 1 for about six or eight months and then it dropped down to No. 2. It stayed No. 2 from then on in. Then I come back with *In the Mood for Love, Hobo Blues, Crawling King Snake*. Modern Records.

So Besman got the contract with Modern Records?
Yeah. I see him right now. He's really gentleman. He's down in L.A. Every time I go there, I gotta go over to his house.

When you first went into the studio, I've heard the story that you had a plywood board, that you kept the rhythm on. Whose idea was that?
Yeah, that's true. Bernie Besman's.

Had you ever done that before?
Yeah, but not in a studio. Just around house parties. I hadn't never used plywood, but I used just a ordinary floor, you know. That was his idea. When I made *Boogie Chillen*, wasn't no drums on that – just my feet and my guitar.

Did they run your voice and guitar through an echo chamber back then?
Yes, on one record – *In the Mood*.

Who's your favorite blues singer?
In the late years, listenin' to the blues singers – I listen to blues records a lot. Albert King is my idol. Yeah, me and him are really good friends. It ain't that, but I don't know, it's just somethin' about his voice and guitar that gets to me, and Little Walter, but he's gone. I do a lot of his stuff.

People never seem to have heard much about blues in Detroit before your records came out. When you got there, were there many blues singers around there?
They was there but there wasn't nothin' happenin', you know. I'm really the one that started the blues in Detroit. Yeah, I started it rolling in Detroit. I made the blues in Detroit.

Do you remember who some of the other people were?
There was a lot of them around there. Boogie Woogie Red, and Eddie Kirkland, Eddie Burns, Little Sonny, oh, a whole bunch of 'em. Baby Boy Warren.

Calvin Frazier? Was he there?
Oh, yeah. Calvin Frazier. And Little George. It's a whole lot of them that never did get a record, you know, or recognized and get known. They was good, too, but they just never could get off the ground.

In the '50s you were recording for a lot of different labels under different names.
Like Birmingham Sam and Texas Slim. Yes, *every* record company wanted me to do something for 'em, you know! If they had the money, I had the time. We'd just change the name. So now I quit doin' that. I don't do that no more.

Was there any trouble over that? It would seem that there would be.
No, it wasn't no trouble, no. Not any trouble at all. I think some of 'em knew it but they didn't do nothin' about it. You can't do that now. You do that now, they, well they're scared of each other. If they get some artist and do that, they're afraid the other company gonna sue them. They're scared of gettin' sued. So they ain't gonna do it. The first thing they ask you, Is you under contract with somebody?" So many little labels out now. I reckon it's about a million labels.

When you started going on the road, did you take a band with you? Or did you go by yourself?
I went by myself. Course, sometimes we'd pick up a band, sometimes we wouldn't. Sometimes I'd just play by myself.

Did you play clubs on these real early tours? Or did you play taverns, or theaters, or what?
Well, these clubs, you know it was clubs and taverns. I played some sophisticated clubs, back there then. Because the record was so big they were puttin' me in these big, big places. Big nightclubs. Sometimes I'd be scared to death because I hadn't never played in front of that many people. And concerts – I'd be playin' in front of 30 to 40,000 people. Just sittin' there by myself. I enjoyed it then.

Were you working any special clubs around Detroit very much?
Yeah, a club called the Club Caribbean. The Apex Bar, And some other clubs I done forget the name of 'em. But them two, I knew I worked at all the time.

What was Hastings Street like back then?
Oh, it was rough. Wide open. Anything goes.

How would it compare to the South or West Side of Chicago?
Well, it was a street that was way, way more known than the South Side streets. I think that street was known more than any other street in the United States. Anywhere, everywhere you'd go, you could hear people talkin' about Hastings Street. Any city you'd go in there, that street's known. I helped made it known, too.

continued from page 4

Yeah, Henry's Swing Club.
Yeah, I used to play at that club. Well that guy used to keep me in there, 'cause I really made his club famous when I made that song on Henry's Swing Club. People would come there, man, and all the time – everybody that came to town, they would hear of that club all across the country, because they'd come right there. He'd just let me play there, he even gave me good money. It was just *my club*. Whenever I wanted it. But that was a really famous street. Everything went on on Hastings Street. Anything you name, was on Hastings Street.

Pretty wide open, huh?
Wide open! Now it's an expressway now. The Chrysler Expressway. But they went to 12th Street, most of 'em. But still it's not like Hastings. Detroit ain't what it used to be. It got so rough now.

Do you remember when you first got a band together?
Yeah. In Detroit. James Watkins and Eddie Burns, Thomas Whitehead and Boogie Woogie Red. Then later on we got another band together and I got rid of that band: Johnny Hooks, and then I still had Tom Whitehead. Jimmy Miller. Johnny Hooks played tenor sax. Otis Finch played tenor sax. I had two horns, bass drum and two guitars – I had a pretty good-sized band then. We used to call ourselves the Boogie Ramblers. That was right there in Detroit and I was going pretty strong then.

How about Eddie Kirkland? He played on a lot of your records.
Oh, yeah. Now he was the first guy I played with. We used to go on the road by ourself with just two guitars – just me and him traveled all over the country. Throw my guitar in the trunk, or in the car, we'd just sit there and drive, and I had a brand new car, burn one up and buy another one [laughs]. Yeah, me and Eddie Kirk, you know, I think about those days. I spent all of my best years right there in Detroit. Yeah, they was really good to me, you know, those days, and I'm still blessed. Still feel good and I'm still thankful for a lot of things. Then and now too. I have to give credit to my public, you know. Thanks to the public.

Did you work very much with Earl Hooker? Was he ever in Detroit with you?
My cousin? Yeah. I worked a lot with him.

When you started playing with a good-sized band, did you ever have a preference for having horns in the band or a harmonica in the band? I know they put a harmonica on some of your Vee-Jay things – Jimmy Reed recorded with you.
Yeah, well, I had a preference, yeah. It was a hard decision to make because I used to use horns when I first started and I always was crazy about a good horn player. But after harps got famous, I had a preference to harmonicas. But until recently I really found out how important a harmonica was, I had preference to a horn. But after hearin' Little Walter and all them other people, how good they was, how they sound, then I had preference to a harmonica. But until then, I didn't.

Did you think it was hard for people to accompany you?
Yeah. Because when I first started out, I was accompanying myself. And anybody accompany theirself for so long, you got to work at it a long time to get to learn how to let the other musicians follow you because you ain't payin' them any attention, you're just doing your thing. And then you have to work with it to learn to go along with the other musicians. Took me a long time to do that. And still learnin'. I can do it, but when I first started, it was hard for me to play with other musicians. With two guitars, yes, I was used to playin' with them. But if it's a band, no. But they wanted to play with me so and, you know, they'd follow and follow me, and just wherever I go, they go right there. It wasn't no static or nothin', because they wanted to play with me. But I finally had to get into that, so I did.

Eddie Taylor was with you, too, on some of your records. Did you know Eddie down South?
No. I knowed him when I first got up in Chicago. I been knowin' him back in the '50s. So it's been close to about 20 years or more. Him and Jimmy Reed and all of 'em. So he was Jimmy Reed's main man. I mean on records, you know, he made "that sound." I guess everybody know that he made that Jimmy Reed sound for so many years. Yeah, he made a lot of sounds on me. Yea, well practically everything I did [for Vee-Jay], he was on it, wasn't he? I'd tell 'em, "Well, if I can't get Eddie, I'd rather just wait until I can get him, you know." This company, well, (Ewart) Abner and Calvin (Carter), they drove to Detroit and picked me up when I first got on their label. I was with a company called Modern Records, and when my contract expired with them, Abner called me. He said, "Well, look, we're coming to get you. We ain't gonna depend on you comin' on your

continued from page 5

own 'cause you may not get here. We're gonna drive there and pick you up." I said, "OK." They drove there in a old Oldsmobile, him and Calvin, they picked me up, and they come up there. They had that old place there on Michigan Avenue. They had a regular record store there, too. I think 22nd & Michigan, that's where they started at. After about a couple or three years – might not have been that long – when we come up to really makin' 'em some big money, they spread it out and got the big place, you know. But I would say, it was *our* place, me and Jimmy Reed's and all of us. It was our build-up. They hadn't done nothin' with the rest of the guys on there. 'Cause my first hit with them was *Dimples*. *Dimples* and *Baby Lee*, and all those others, so many of my old ones. So after they fell through, I went with ABC and I stayed with them about 10 years.

Would you rather cut records by yourself or with a band?
Both ways. Because now today, we got so many young kids like to boogie. Then we got a lot of old people that like to sit and listen. You got to cut records to sell to the young people buyin' records, you know. So I *can* do 'em both and that's one good thing I can say about myself. A lot of musicians, they have to have a band – they can't play by theirself. I can sit down and do it by myself and then I can do it both ways. Now a long time ago, years back, it worked out perfect like that. Like when I first started, everybody liked it. But we got so many young kids comin' up now, they want to dance, they want to buy records, somethin' with a beat to it. So I can make them and then I turn around and make somethin' that's slow-goin' like folk blues. Then you got two different sales.

So, I mean that's the way the business is, but see, sometimes you have to change with the times. If you want to survive. I play a lot of stuff now I really don't particularly like playing.

What in particular don't you like?
You know, just all this fast boogie.

Do you get pretty tired of that real fast boogie stuff?
Yeah, sometimes. Sometime I like it. The kids get into it. And I know what they like. I want to keep eatin', so I got to keep playin', I might not want to play that song. But I notice one thing – I know that Brownie McGhee & Sonny Terry, that's all they do and they work year 'round. But they're different type of clubs, I guess. They play a different circuit. Now, I don't particularly like that kind of (boogie) music but I can do it and I'll do it because the people like it. Most of the people that come to see me are mostly young people. I like playing coffee-houses, and I just sit there, play, you know, and just relaxin' there. It's fun. I can really feel it, too.

If you could play exactly what you wanted to, what kind of stuff would you do?
Exactly what I wanted to do? Get back to the old-time thing. Wouldn't be no strain, no bouncin', no jumpin' up and down. Just sit there, just like I'm havin' a conversation. It's easy. But now I tell you one thing, overseas they like it like that. Overseas they want to hear them blues.

OK, what's a silly question that you get asked all the time, so we won't ask it?
Well, No. 1, the first thing they want to know, how old you is, how long you been in the world. [Laughs.] I say, "Is that gonna do you any good?" "Is that gonna make you feel any better? Or is that gonna put any money in your pocket or somethin'?" I say I'm just like Jack Benny 'cause I'm 39.

You think your music has changed over the years?
No, I got the same basic thing I always had. I'm playin' the same thing I was playin' way back there. But I got it dressed up with a lot of stuff built around it. But I still got the basic bottom. I know what the kids want: they want that big boogie beat. So I have to go along with 'em. But I still like the basic thing that I do.

Reprinted by permission of Living Blues and Jim and Amy O'Neal.

Notes On The Transcriber

During the past few years Richard DeVinck has transcribed guitar tablature songbooks of various recording artists, including "Eric Clapton," "Jimi Hendrix," "Jane's Addiction," and "Nirvana." Richard has always looked upon music as "food for the spirit," having been surrounded by a musical family.

His association with the guitar began in his late teens -- what he often refers to as his "Drop the Needle Period." Unlike today, there were little or no note-for-note guitar transcriptions available. Like most young guitar students and enthusiasts of the late 70s, Richard learned Rock's ABC's by painstakingly dropping the needle of his turntable onto a particular "lick" or "riff" and then figuring out a "reasonable" fingering for it.

It was at The University of California, Los Angeles where Richard received formal training in both the mechanics of music theory and performance practices. Richard holds a Bachelor of Arts degree and a Master of Fine Arts degree, both in guitar performance.

Since his graduation from UCLA, he has been combining his talents into the product you have before you -- a detailed "blueprint" of guitar music of the highest degree. It is Mr. DeVinck's sincere hope that these transcriptions will prove valuable to its reader and save him or her from the tedious task of dropping needles on vinyl.

SELECTED DISCOGRAPHY

The following CD albums were used for these transcriptions. All are the original Detroit Recordings and all feature excellent sound. They are a must for any Hooker fan.

John Lee Hooker - 40th Anniversary Album
DCC Compact Classics #042

John Lee Hooker - The Ultimate Collection: 1948-1990
Rhino Records #R2-70572

John Lee Hooker - Half A Stranger
Mainstream Records #MDCD-903

John Lee Hooker - Cold Chills
Official Records #86065 (Import)

John Lee HOOKER

PERFORMANCE NOTES

Getting a feel for John Lee Hooker's strumming technique will take some practice, careful listening to his recordings, as well as some insight into the following Hooker "basics." Whether playing solo or accompanied, Hooker's signature foot stomps on each quarter-note beat provide a strong sense of rhythmic stability. The basic pulse (usually a shuffle "groove") happens on the upbeats. While tapping out quarter-notes with his foot, John Lee often "slaps" the low strings on each beat with his R.H. thumb. This slapping technique (indicated in TAB by bracketed frets) is achieved by simultaneously strumming the low strings and quickly landing on the strings with the heel of the R. H. thumb. The index finger (sometimes middle or ring finger) backstrokes the high strings on the upbeats. In other words, the thumb and foot mark the downbeats and the fingers sound the accented upbeats with a relaxed swing feel. Sometimes the slapping sound is produced by the left hand instead of the right hand by slapping the 2nd finger across the strings (usually the 3rd fret from the nut or capo) to produce a mute (marked in TAB by an X.) Don't get too hung up on striking the exact strings indicated in each transcription. The important thing is to achieve the rhythmic "feel."

Like Lightnin' Hopkins and a few other bluesmen, Hooker's phrasing does not conform to a standard 4/4 time signature (4/4 often alternates with 6/4, 5/4, 3/4, and 2/4). The structure is determined by Hooker's vocals and chord changes. When backing Hooker, other guitarists often had to anticipate John Lee's chord changes since he not always restricted himself to a traditional 12-bar format. The barlines in the following transcriptions are merely "guidelines" to help the reader keep his/her place. It might be more helpful not to count at all but rather ignore the time signatures and just tap with one's foot and "feel" the count.

ENJOY!

Richard DeVinck
Transcriber

THE NOTATION

Each guitar part is written in both musical notation and guitar tablature.

The tablature tells you which strings should be played at which frets. The six lines of the staff correspond to the strings of the guitar, first string at the top, and the numbers written on the lines indicate which frets should be fingered.

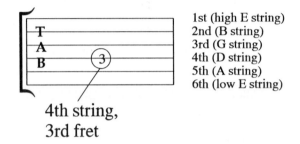

4th string, 3rd fret

1st (high E string)
2nd (B string)
3rd (G string)
4th (D string)
5th (A string)
6th (low E string)

The numbers in the tablature staff should be played with the same rhythm that is written in the music notation staff. (if you're unfamiliar with musical notation, the best plan is to listen to and play along with the recording of the song.) Numbers that are stacked on top of one another should be fingered and played simultaneously as a chord.

Left hand fingering has not been indicated. If you play through a line two or three times, the correct (that is, easiest) fingering should become apparent.

Blues is repetitive: that's part of its charm. There are symbols used throughout to indicate repeating the previous measure, or the previous two measures.

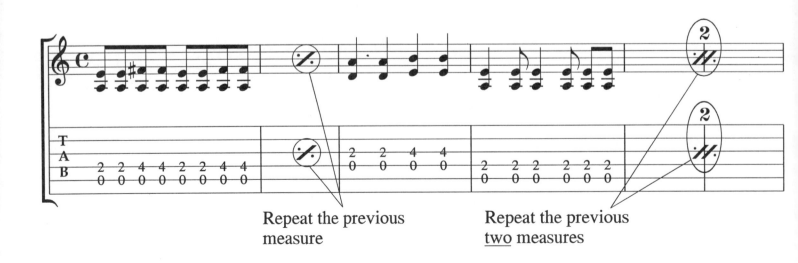

Repeat the previous measure

Repeat the previous two measures

Here is the tablature for some common guitar technique:

BENDS - Finger the string at the fret shown and bend it upwards to produce the note that would ordinarily be heard at the fret number in parenthesis. This usually occurs on the first three strings. Pre-bends are notated in tablature and musical notation in the same manner as the standard bend, however they are indicated with the word "pre-bend". In the case of pre-bends, the string is bent before the string is struck. Quarter ($\frac{1}{4}$) bends are indicated in both musical notation and tablature as an upward slur above the note / fret.

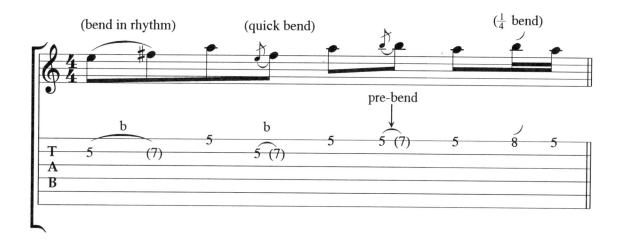

Unless otherwise paired with slurs or footnotes, parenthetic fret numbers / notes indicate "ghost-notes"- very faint pitches produced either with left or right hand.

HAMMER-ONS - Finger the string at the fret shown and produce the next note not by picking it with the right hand, but by hammering a finger of your left hand onto the indicated fret.

PULL-OFFS - Finger the string simultaneously at the fret shown and at the next fret shown. Pick the first note, and produce the next note by plucking the string with the left-hand finger you're pulling off.

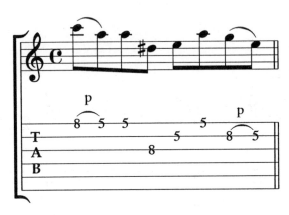

SLIDES - Finger the string at the fret shown and, without lifting your finger, slide up or down to the next indicated fret.

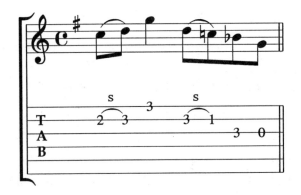

If no fret number is shown before the slide, start a fret or two away and slide quickly to the indicated fret. Or slide away from the indicated fret to an undetermined fret, lifting your finger as you go to mute the string.

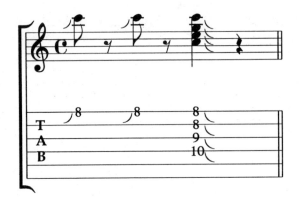

Any of these slides can be performed on single strings or with whole chords.

BABY, HOW CAN YOU DO IT?

Transcribed Off The Album "John Lee Hooker's 40th Anniversary Album"

Guitar Tablature Transcription
by
Richard De Vinck

Words and Music by
John Lee Hooker and Bernard Besman

Fast Boogie Shuffle

Triplet Feel

* Open A Tuning (⑥ = E, ⑤ = A, ④ = E, ③ = A, ② = C♯, ① = E)
  Capo at 3rd fret
† Meter determined by Vcls. and Gtr. 1

** Standard Tuning (⑥ = E, ⑤ = A, ④ = D, ③ = G, ② = B, ① = E)
  Capo at 3rd fret

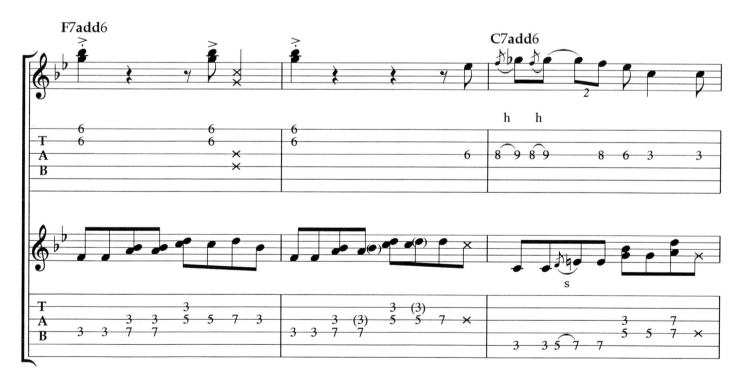

© 1989 LA CIENEGA MUSIC
This arrangement © 1992 LA CIENEGA MUSIC
All Rights Reserved

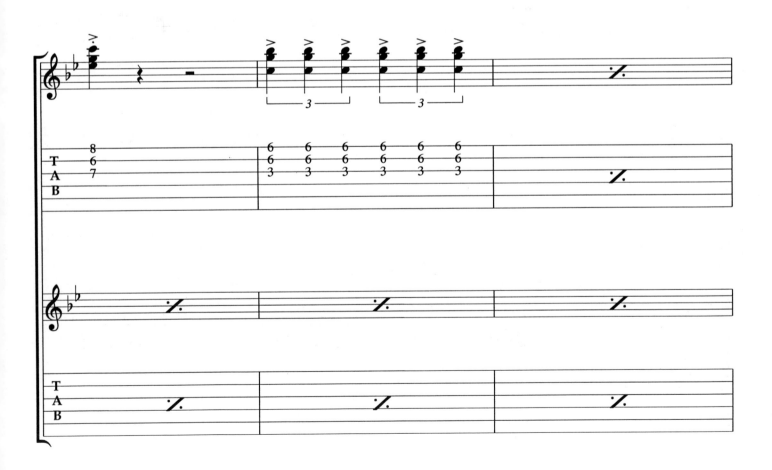

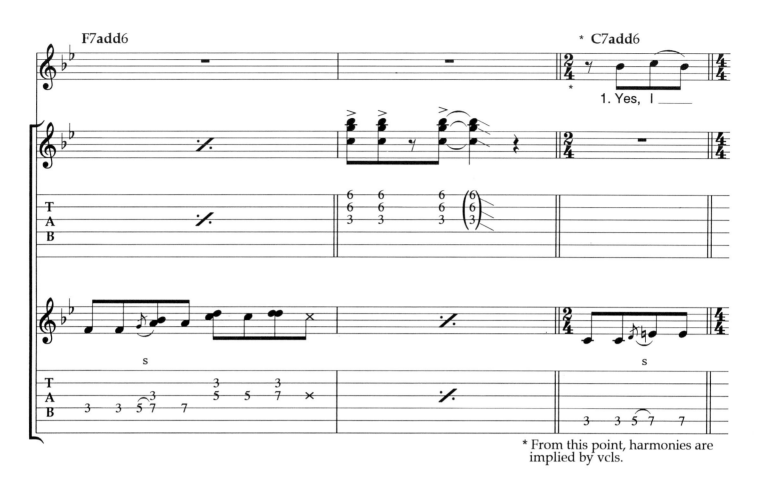

* From this point, harmonies are implied by vcls.

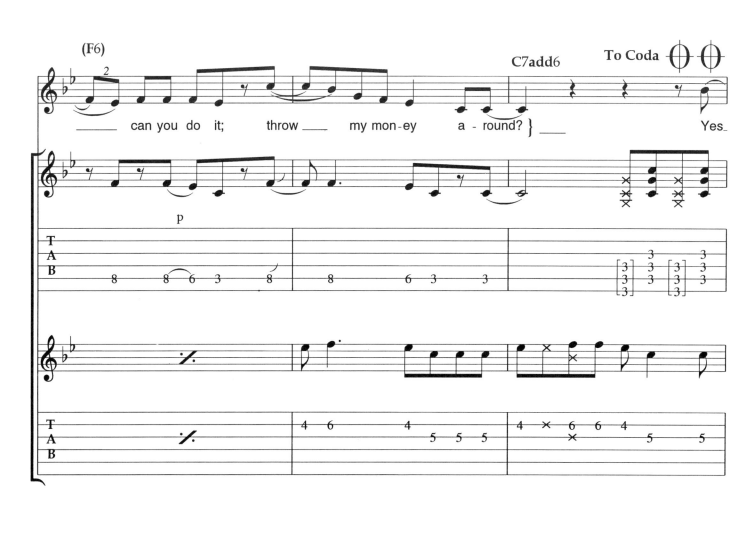
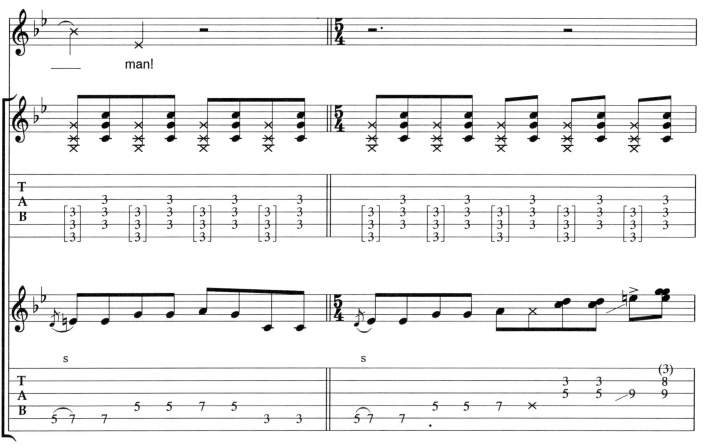

26

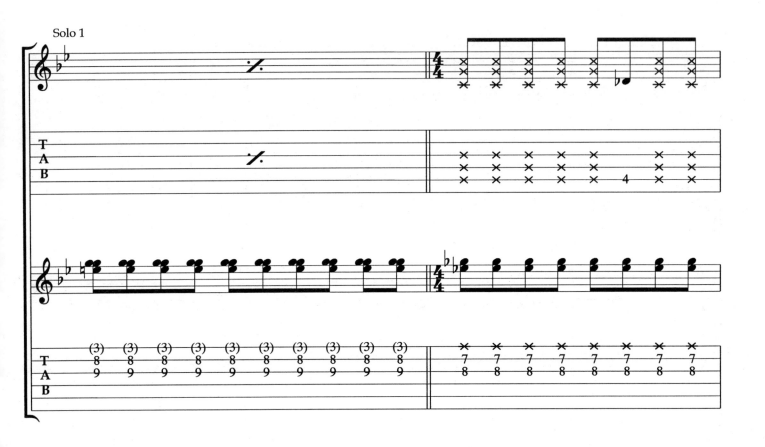

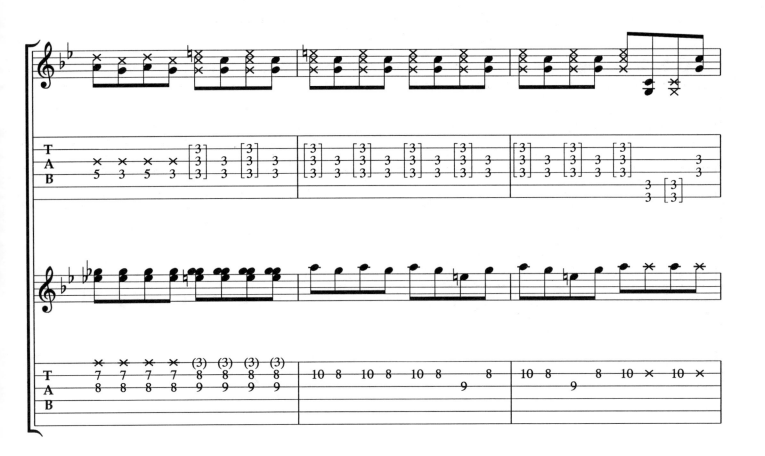

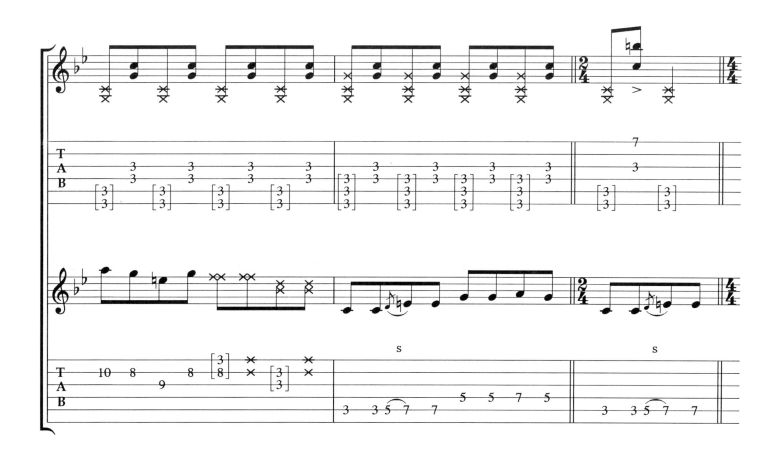

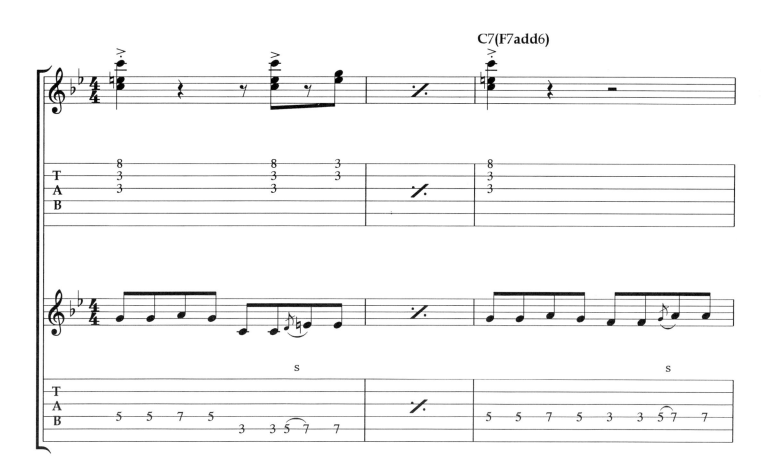

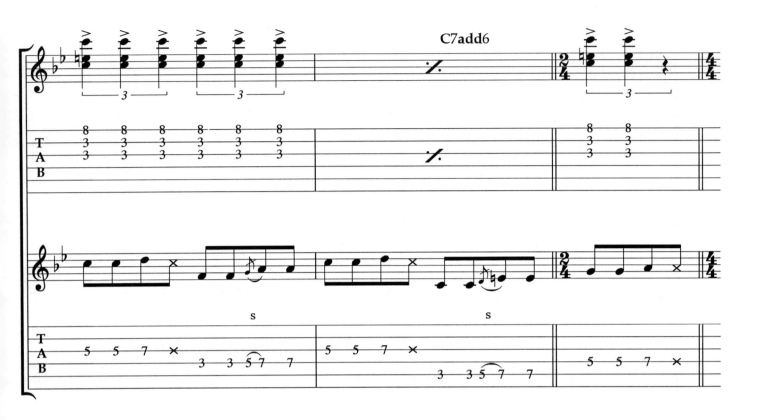
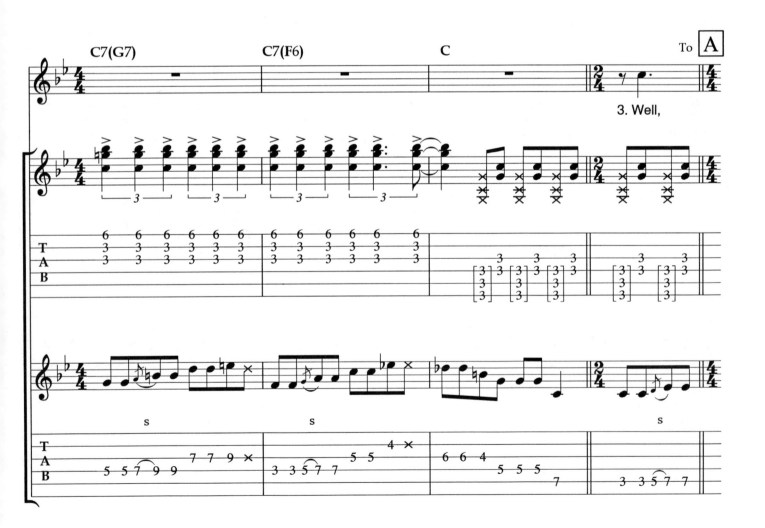

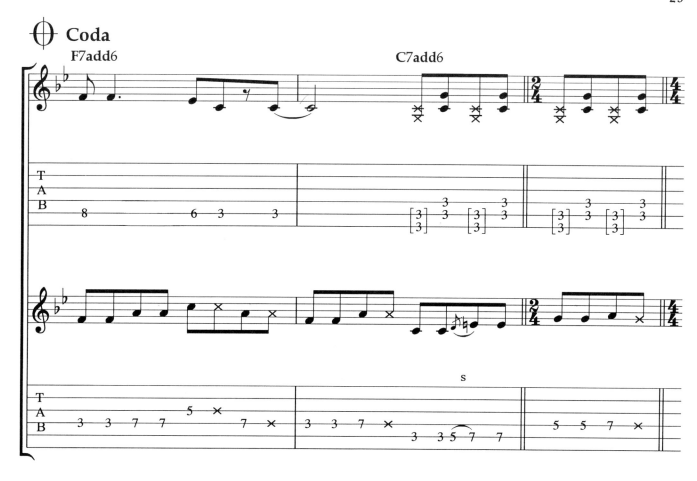
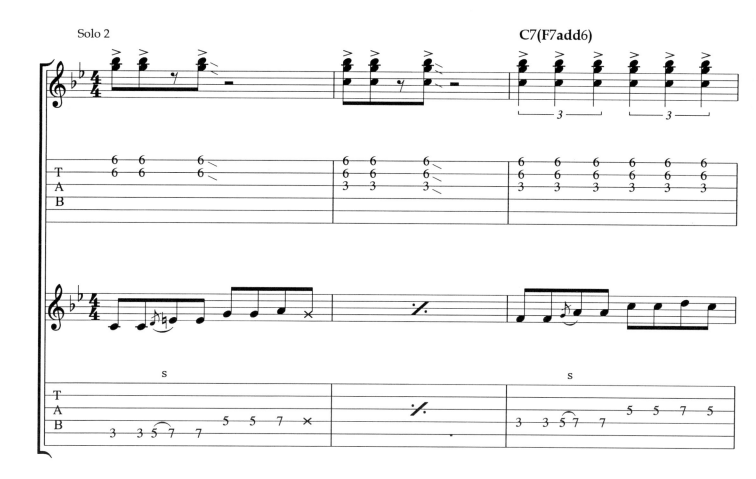

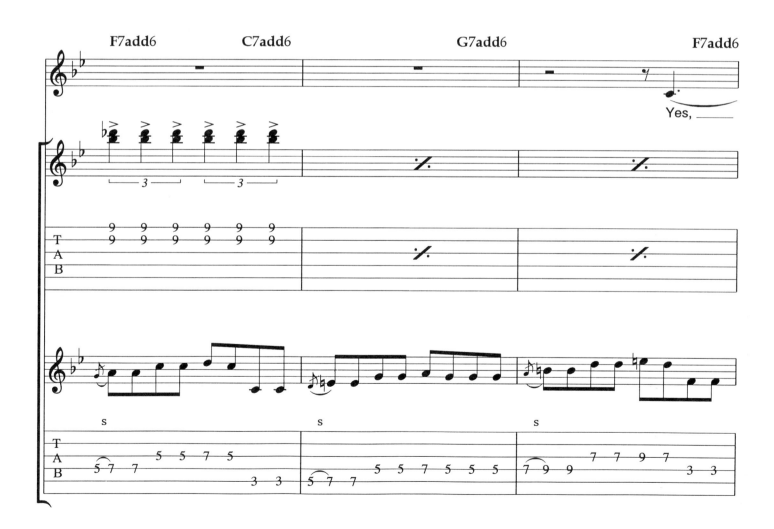

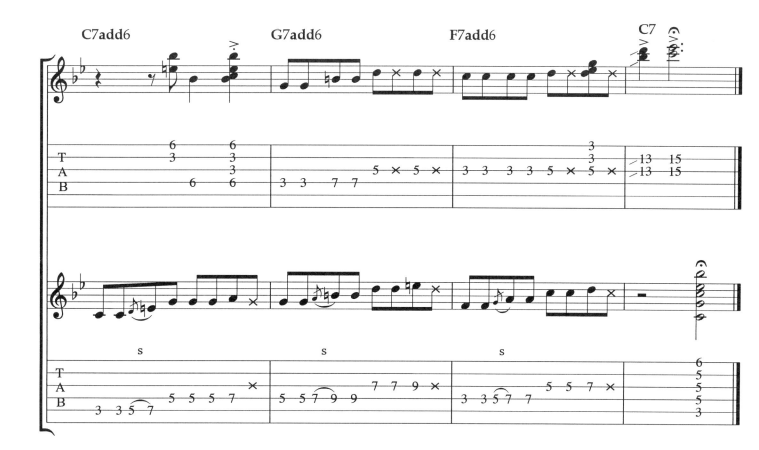

BOOGIE CHILLEN'

Transcribed Off The Album "John Lee Hooker : The Ultimate Collection (1948 - 1990)"

Guitar Tablature Transcription
by
Richard De Vinck

Words and Music by
John Lee Hooker and Bernard Besman

Open A Tuning:

⑥ = E ④ = E ② = C#
⑤ = A ③ = A ① = E

* Capo at 2nd Fret

Moderately Fast Boogie Shuffle

Triplet Feel

* 2nd fret indicates open stgs. ** Brackets indicate a "choppy" attack, achieved by dropping the palm of R.H. onto the strgs. with each strum.

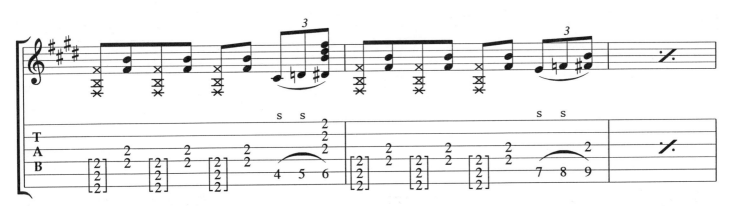

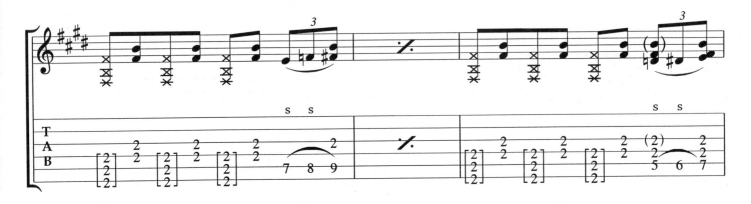

© 1967 LA CIENEGA MUSIC
This arrangement © 1992 LA CIENEGA MUSIC
All rights Reserved

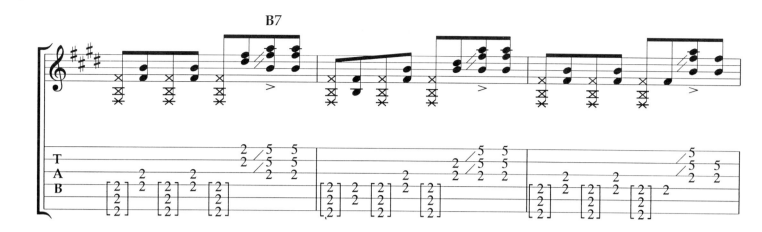

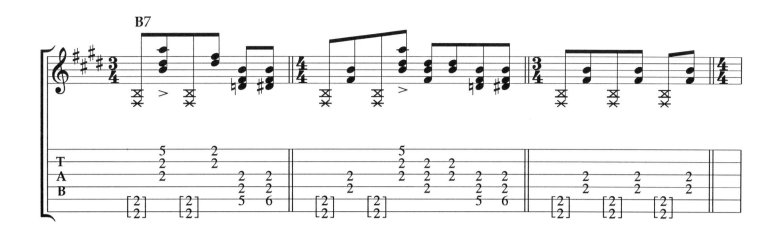
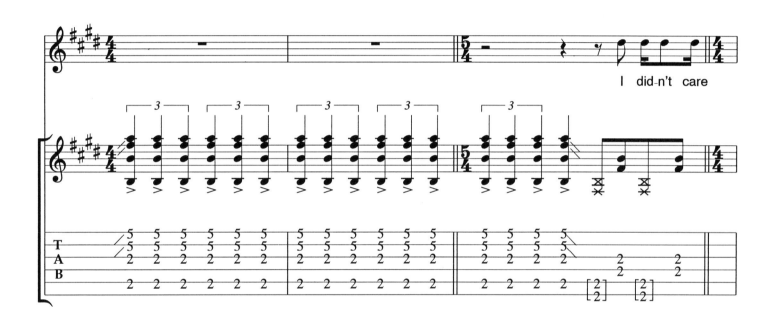
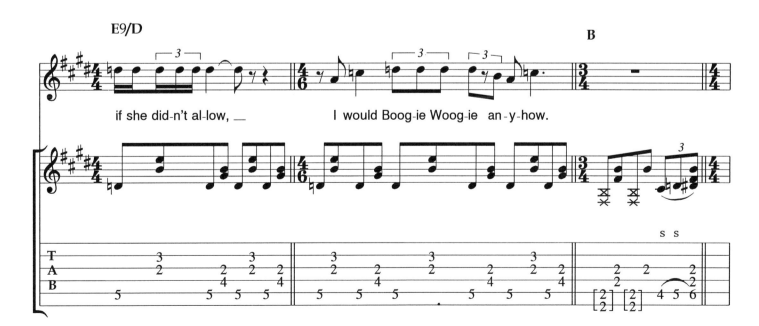

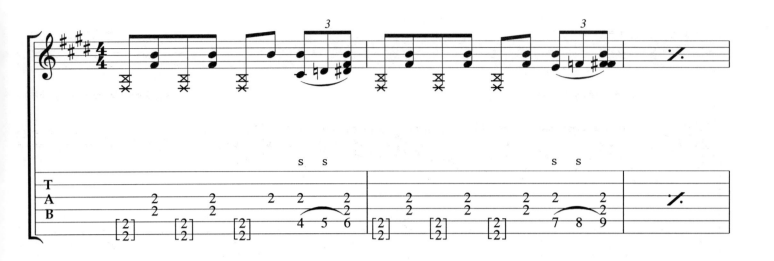
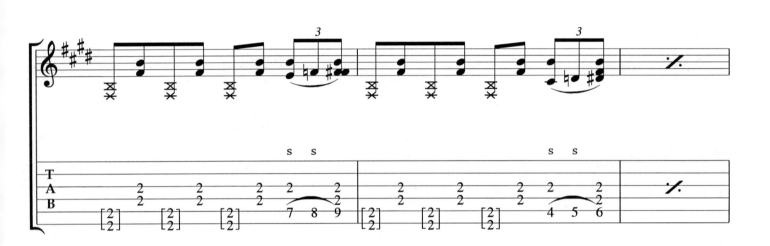
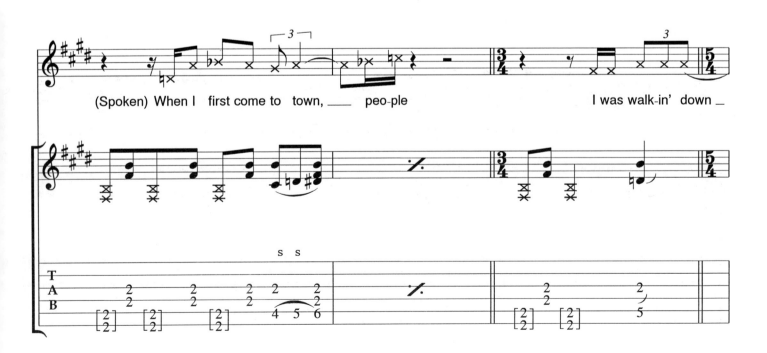

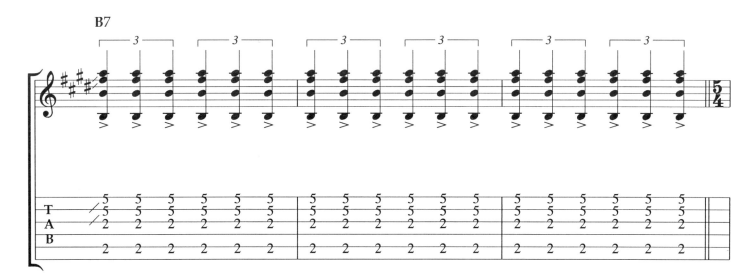

Boog-ie Chill-en'!

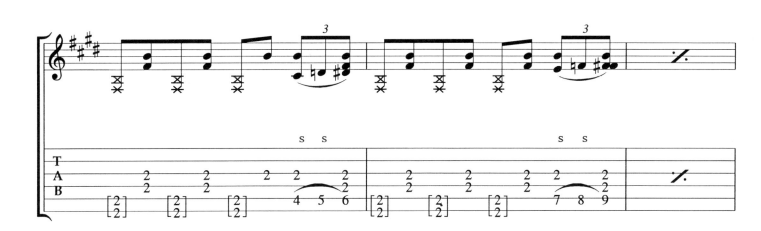

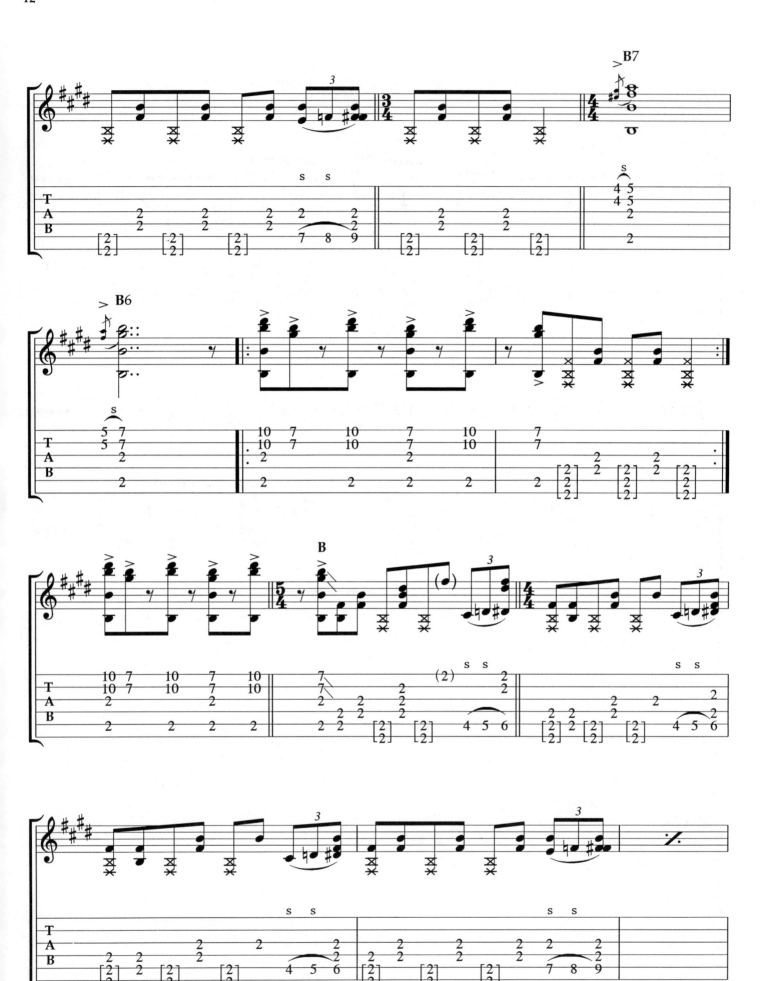

COLD CHILLS ALL OVER ME

Transcribed Off The Album "Cold Chills"

Guitar Tablature Transcription
by
Richard De Vinck

Words and Music by
John Lee Hooker and Bernard Besman

Open E Tuning:

⑥ = E   ④ = E   ② = B
⑤ = B   ③ = G# ① = E

* Capo at 3rd fret

Moderately Slow Blues Shuffle

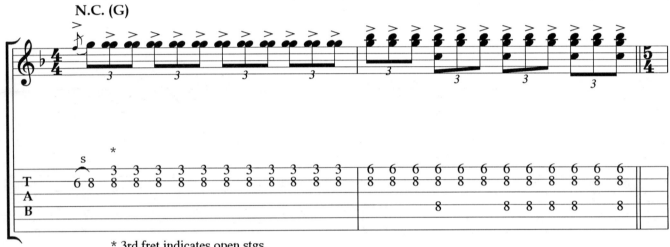

* 3rd fret indicates open stgs.

* Cold Chills,

* Vcls. doubled in unison

© 1952 and renewed 1980 LA CIENEGA MUSIC
This arrangement © 1992 LA CIENEGA MUSIC
All rights Reserved

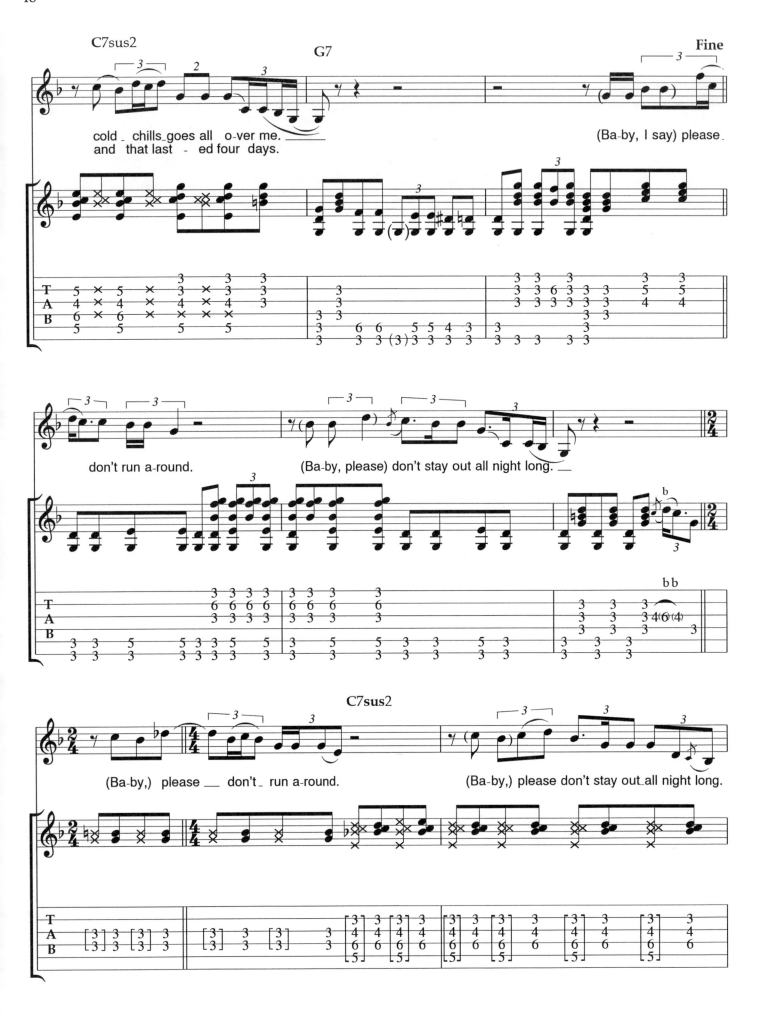

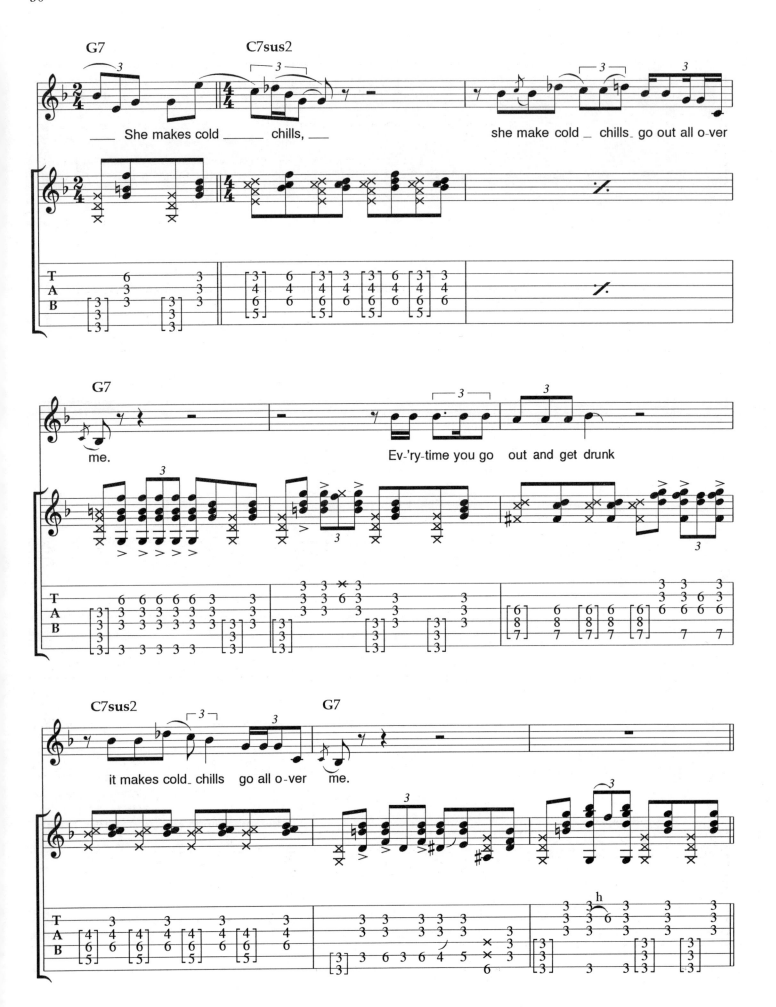

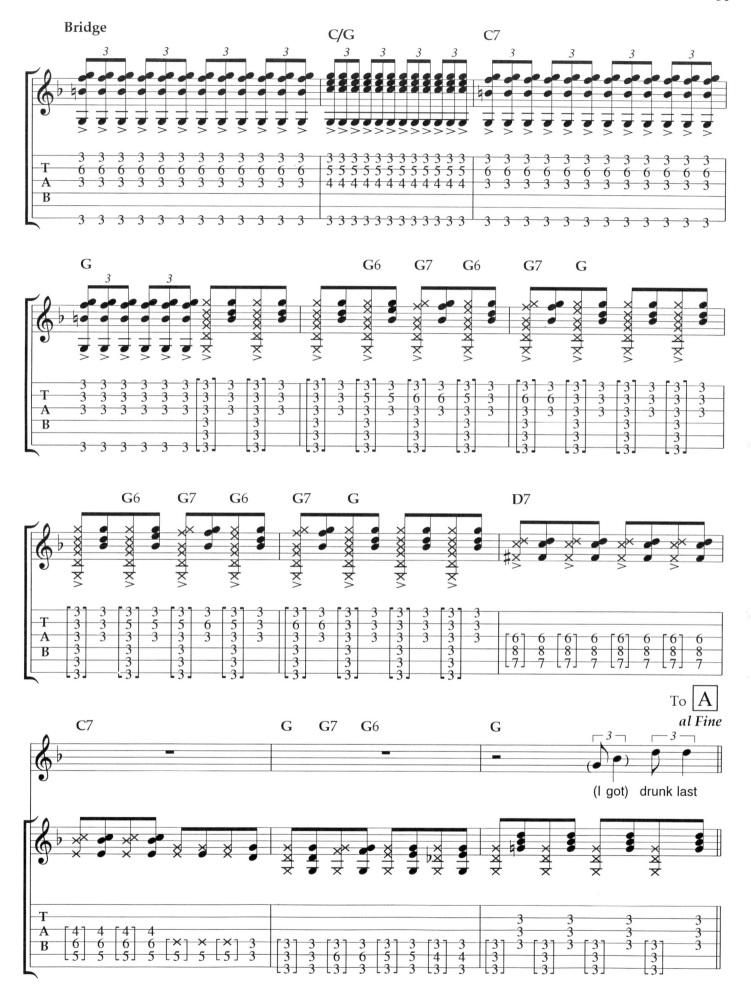

HELLO, BABY
(Don't You Remember Me?)
Transcribed Off The Album "John Lee Hooker's 40th Anniversary Album"

Guitar Tablature Transcription
by
Richard De Vinck

Words and Music by
John Lee Hooker and Bernard Besman

Standard Tuning:
⑥ = E ④ = D ② = B
⑤ = A ③ = G ① = E

* Capo at 2nd fret

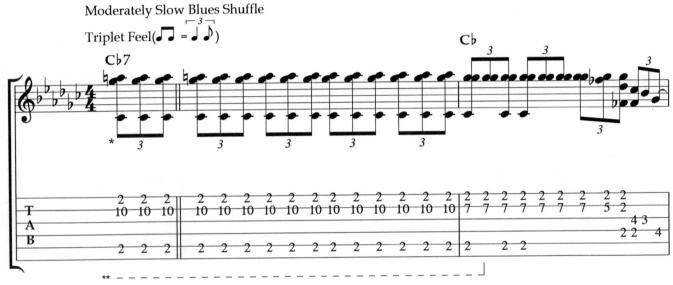

** Cb(open ⑤) barely audible
* Fret 2 indicates open stgs.

© 1977, 1989 LA CIENEGA MUSIC
This arrangement © 1992 LA CIENEGA MUSIC
All rights Reserved

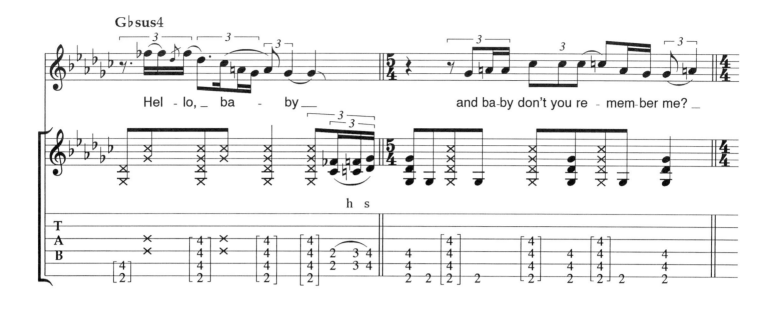

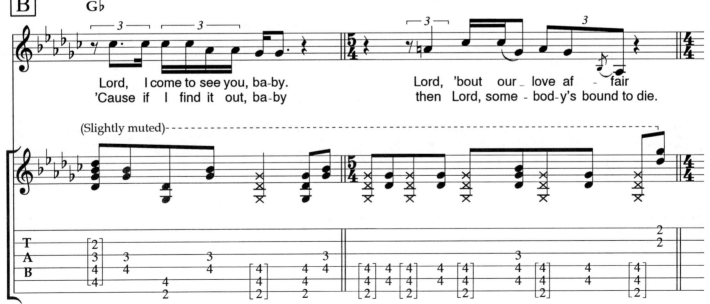

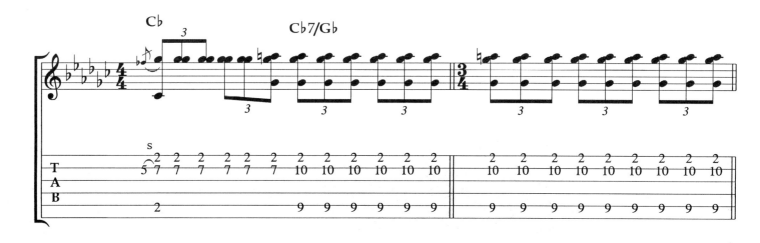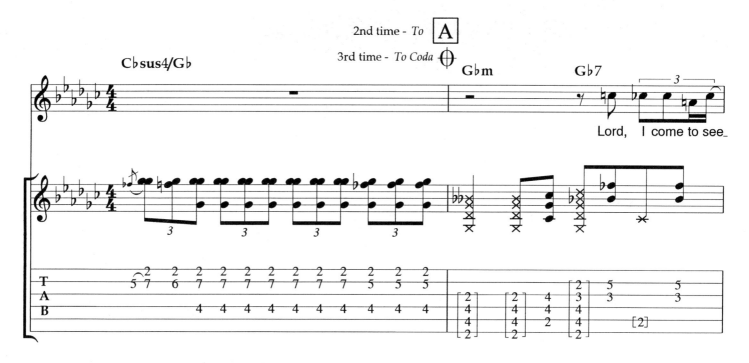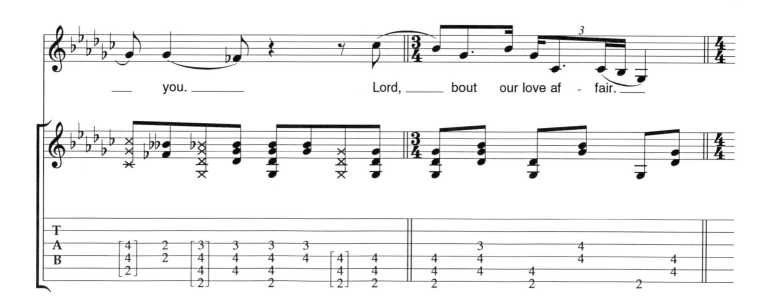

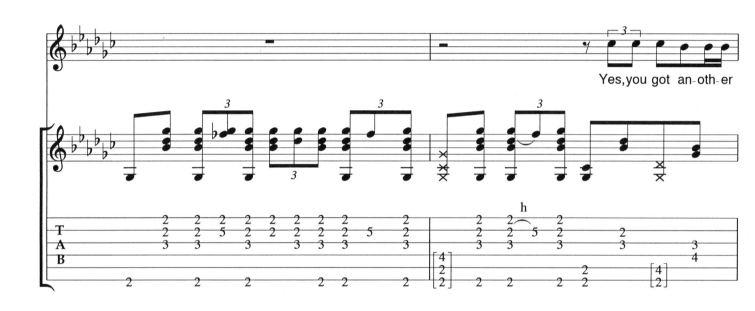

Yes, you got an-oth-er

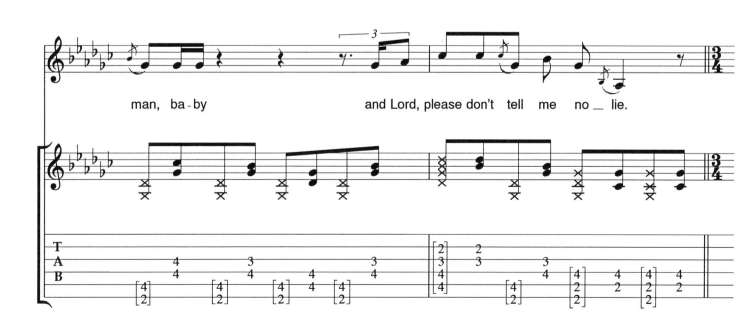

man, ba-by   and Lord, please don't tell me no lie.

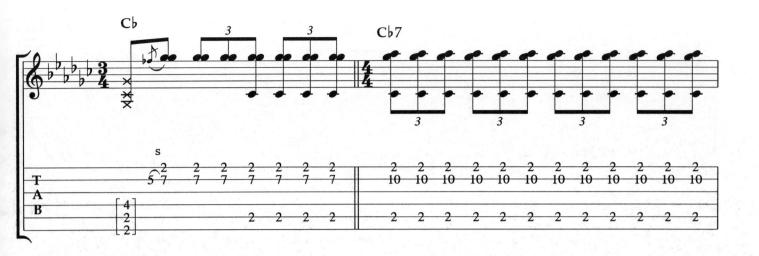
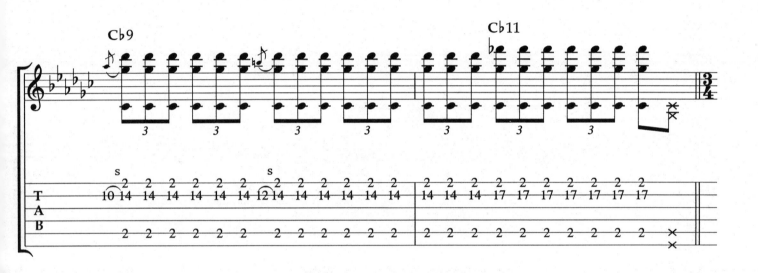

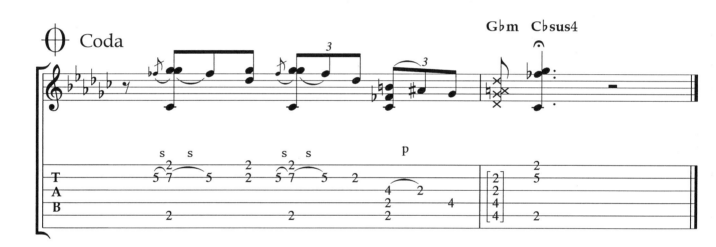

Additional Lyrics

Lord, straighten up, ba-by
'Cause your daddy's comin' home.
Lord, straighten up, ba-by
'Cause your daddy's comin' home to stay.
Lord, straighten up, ba-by
And see thing(s) 'lil' Johnny's way.

I GOT THE KEY
(Key to The Highway)

Transcribed Off The Album "John Lee Hooker's 40th Anniversary Album"

Guitar Tablature Transcription by Richard De Vinck

Words and Music by John Lee Hooker and Bernard Besman

Moderate Blues Shuffle

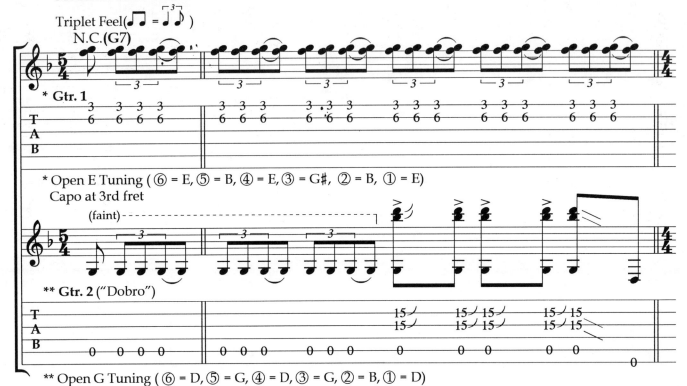

* Open E Tuning (⑥ = E, ⑤ = B, ④ = E, ③ = G♯, ② = B, ① = E)
Capo at 3rd fret

** Open G Tuning (⑥ = D, ⑤ = G, ④ = D, ③ = G, ② = B, ① = D)

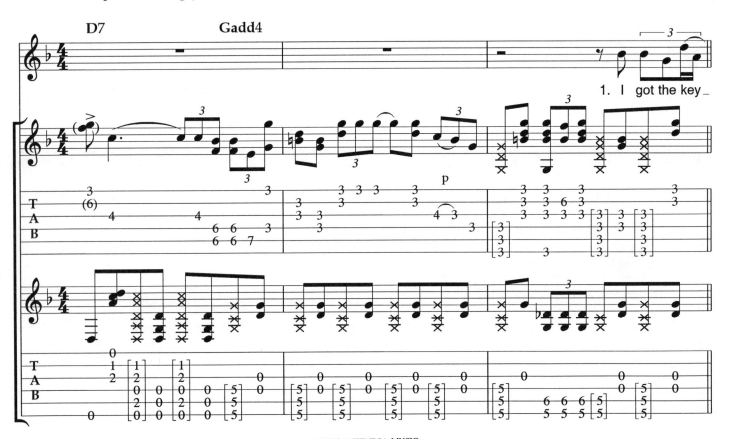

© 1991 LA CIENEGA MUSIC
This arrangement © 1992 LA CIENEGA MUSIC
All Rights Reserved

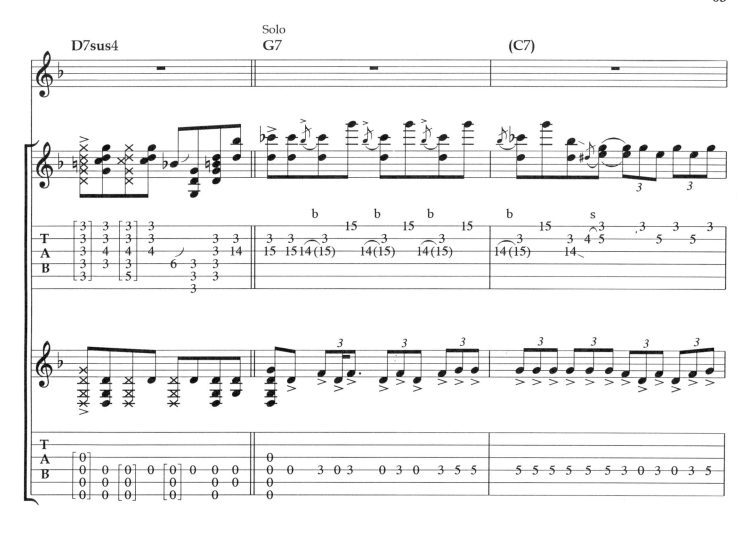
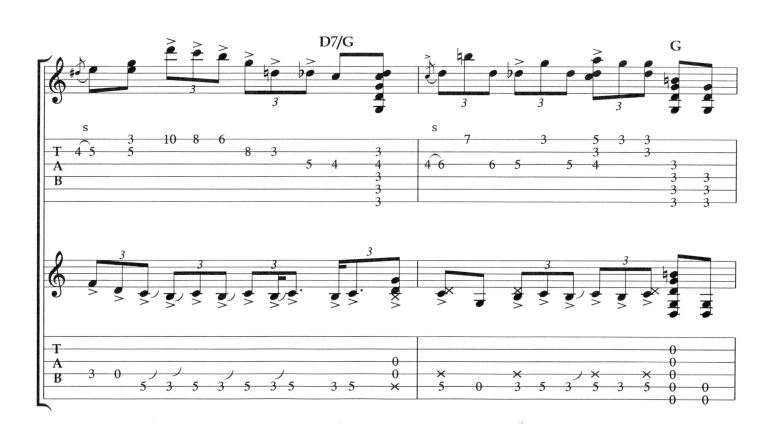

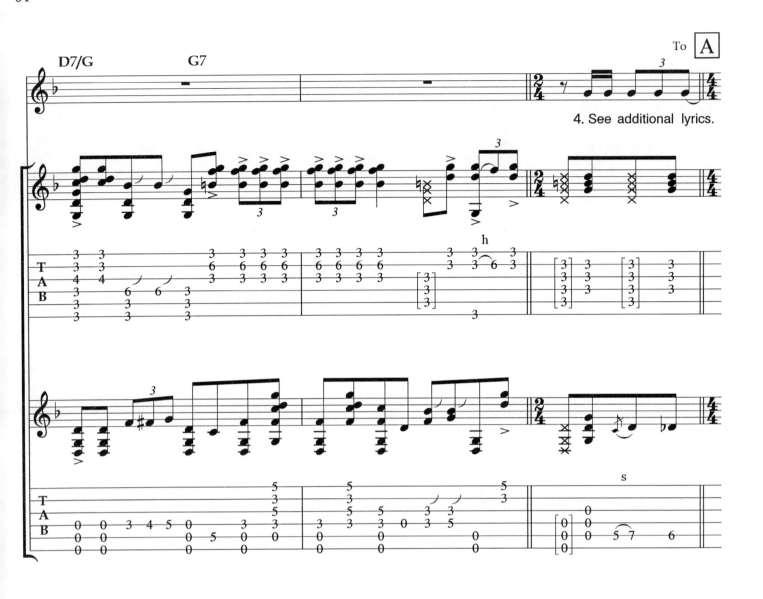

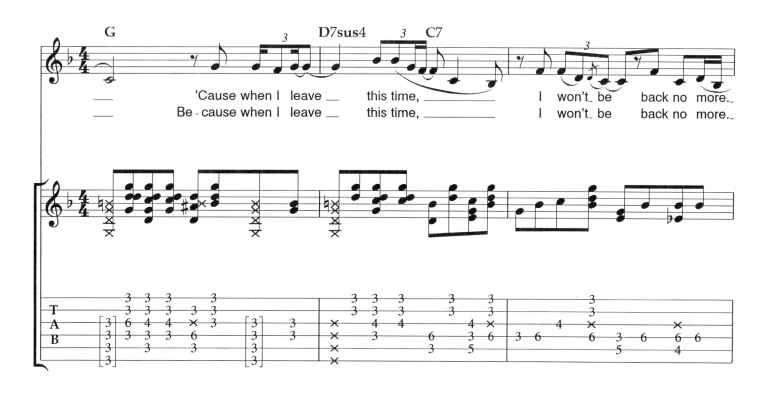
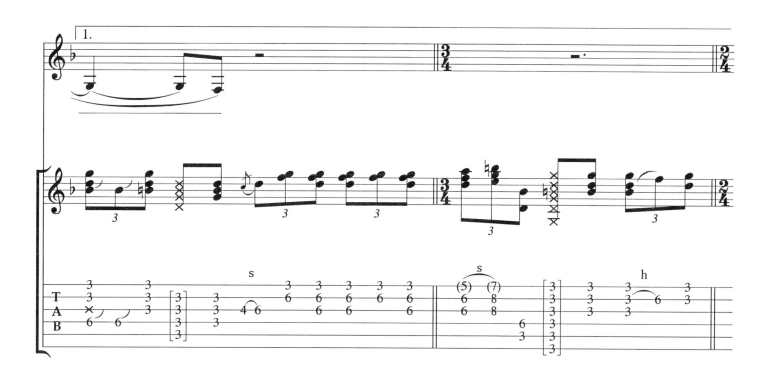

Additional Lyrics

2. Yes, when the moon peep o'r the mountain
   Honey, I'll be on my way.
   I'm gonna roam this highway
   Until the day I die.

3. Just give me one, one more kiss, babe.
   Baby, just before I go.
   Be - cause I'm leavin' this mornin'.
   I won't be back no mo'.

4. So I said,"So long, so long baby.
   Honey, I must say goodbye."
   'Cause when I leave this time
   I won't be back no mo'.

I'M GONNA GIT ME A WOMAN

Transcribed Off The Album "John Lee Hooker's 40th Anniversary Album"

Guitar Tablature Transcription
by
Richard De Vinck

Words and Music by
John Lee Hooker and Bernard Besman

Open A Tuning:

⑥ = E   ④ = E   ② = C#
⑤ = A   ③ = A   ① = E

* Capo at 2nd fret

Moderately Slow Blues Shuffle

* 2nd fret indicates open stgs.

** Brackets indicate a "choppy" attack, achieved by dropping the palm of R.H. onto the strgs. with each strum.

© 1989 LA CIENEGA MUSIC
This arrangement © 1992 LA CIENEGA MUSIC
All rights Reserved

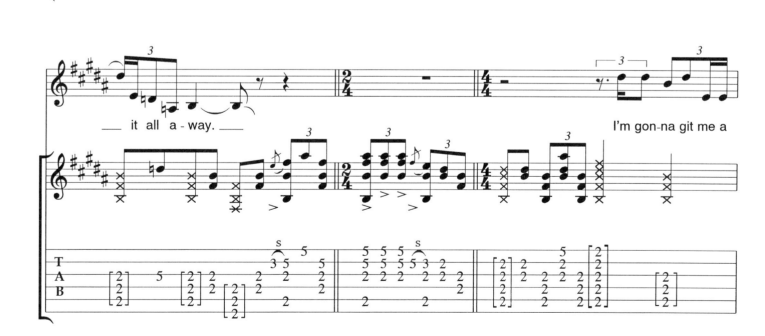

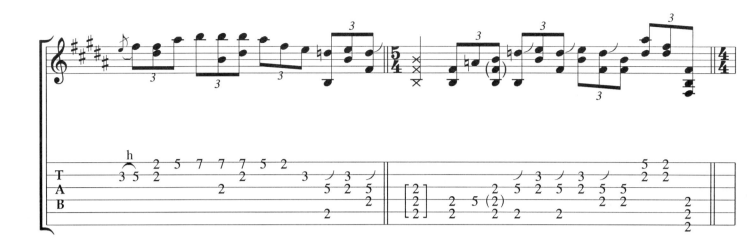
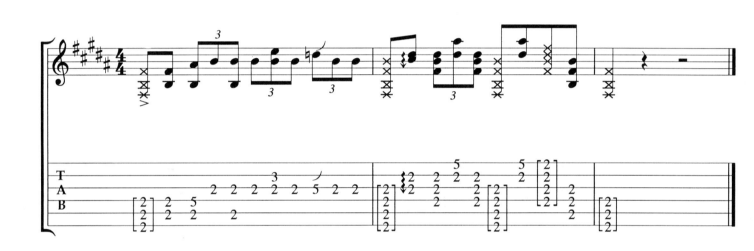

I'M IN THE MOOD

Transcribed Off The Album "John Lee Hooker's 40th Anniversary Album"

Guitar Tablature Transcription
by
Richard De Vinck

Words and Music by
John Lee Hooker and Bernard Besman

Open E Tuning:

⑥ = E   ④ = E   ② = B
⑤ = B   ③ = G# ① = E

* Capo at 3rd fret

Modeate Blues Shuffle

Triplet Feel (♫ = ♪♪)

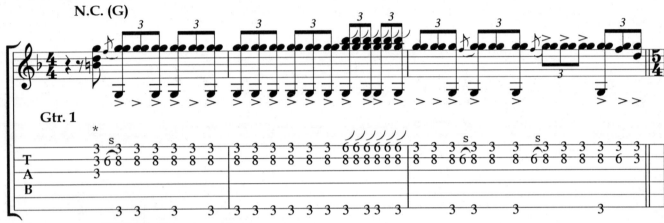

* 3rd fret indicates open stgs.

© 1951 and renewed 1979 LA CIENEGA MUSIC
This arrangement © 1992 LA CIENEGA MUSIC
All rights Reserved

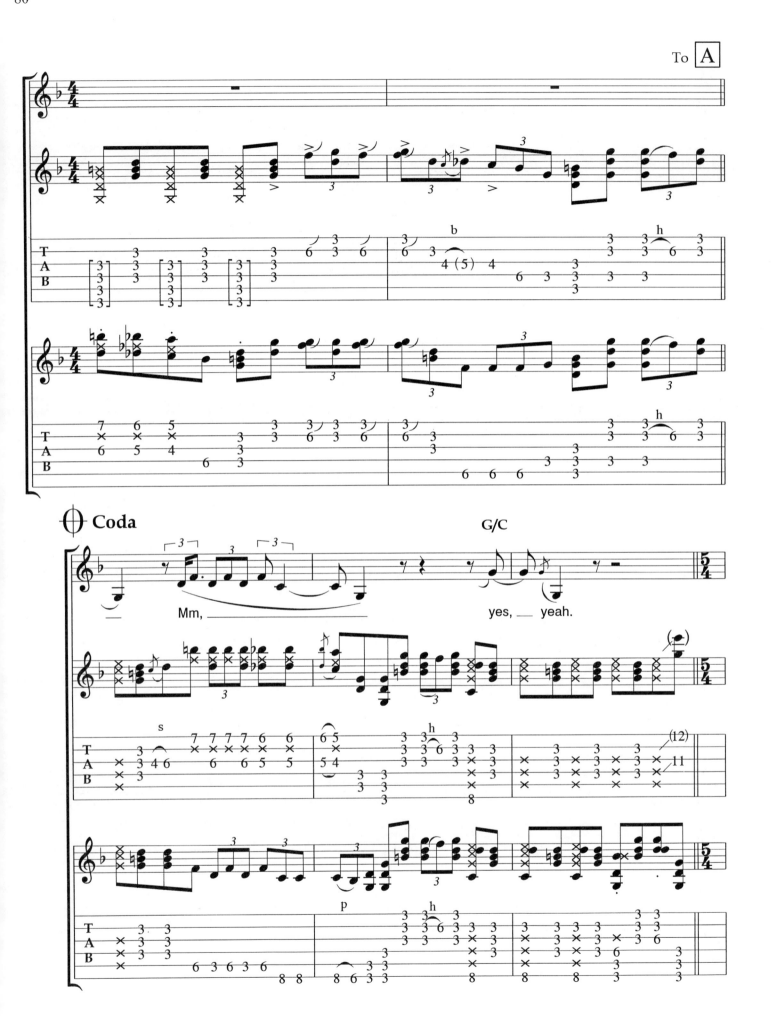

I'm in the mood,

83

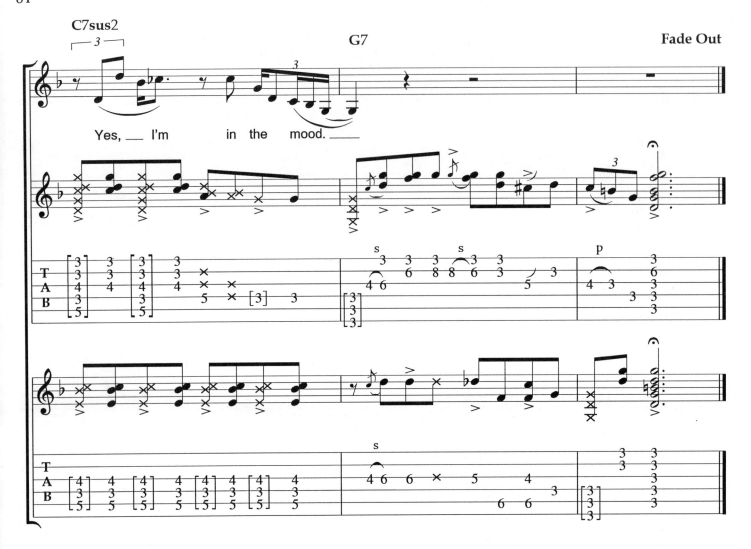

Additional Lyrics

2. If I don't be wit' you baby, God knows
   I sure can't get my thrill.
   If I don't be wit' you baby, God knows
   I don't want no one else. (To Chorus)

3. Yes, My mama told me
   To leave that gal alone.
   But she didn't know, God knows
   What that gal was puttin down. (To Chorus)

   (Chorus)
   I'm in the mood. I'm in the mood.
   I'm in the mood for love
   I'm in the mood. I'm in the mood
   Yes, I'm in the mood.

LET'S TALK IT OVER

Transcribed Off The Album "John Lee Hooker's 40th Anniversary Album"

Guitar Tablature Transcription
by
Richard De Vinck

Words and Music by
John Lee Hooker and Bernard Besman

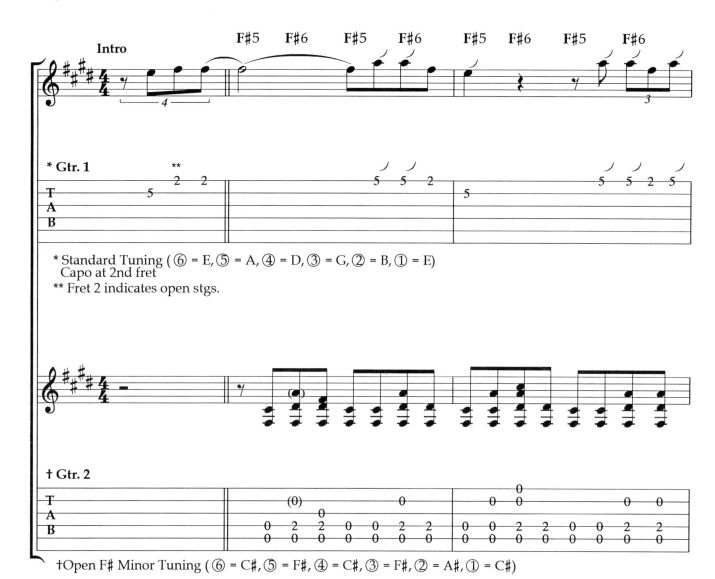

* Standard Tuning (⑥ = E, ⑤ = A, ④ = D, ③ = G, ② = B, ① = E)
  Capo at 2nd fret
** Fret 2 indicates open stgs.

†Open F♯ Minor Tuning (⑥ = C♯, ⑤ = F♯, ④ = C♯, ③ = F♯, ② = A♯, ① = C♯)

© 1954 and renewed 1982 LA CIENEGA MUSIC
This arrangement © 1992 LA CIENEGA MUSIC
All Rights Reserved

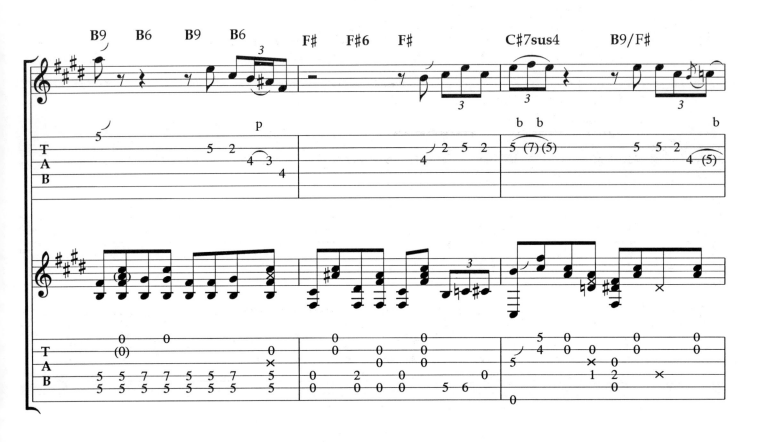

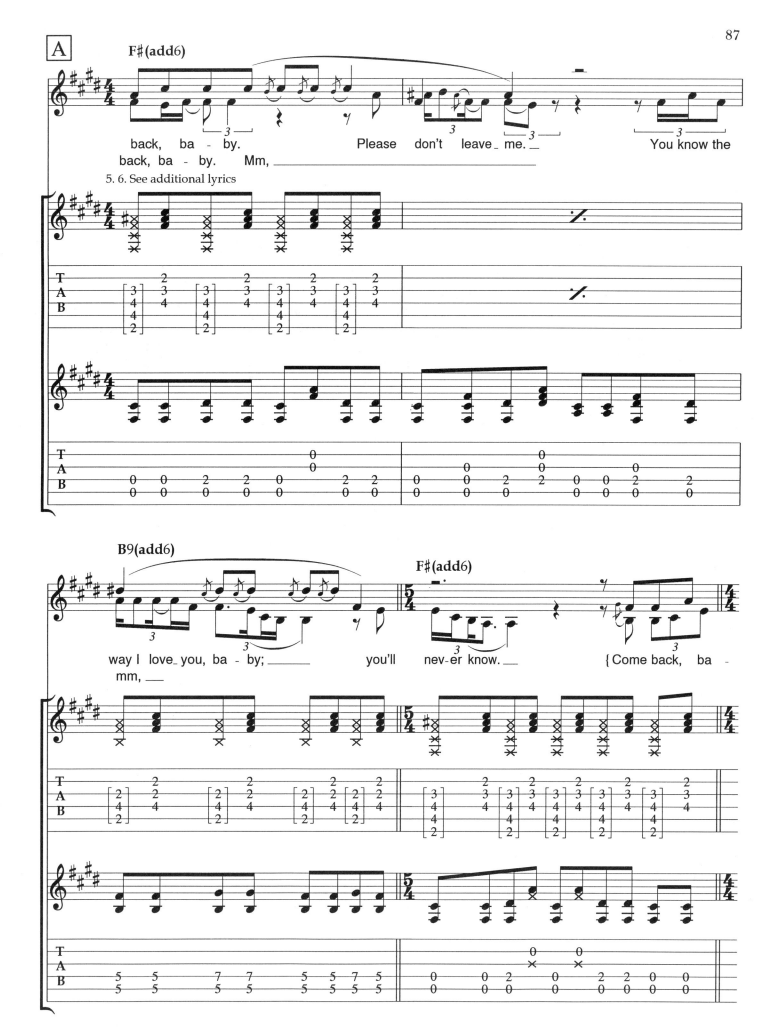

Additional Lyrics

5. My heart is beatin' like a hammer.
   I really can tell
   You've been gone for twenty-four hours baby
   Seems like a thousand years
   Come back baby
   Let's Talk It Over
   One more time

6. You know baby
   This world wasn't made in one day
   Don't pay no attention baby
   To what the people say
   Come back baby
   Let's Talk It Over
   One more time.

IT HURTS ME SO

Transcribed Off The Album "John Lee Hooker's 40th Anniversary Album"

Guitar Tablature Transcription
by
Richard De Vinck

Words and Music by
John Lee Hooker and Bernard Besman

Open E Tuning:
⑥ = E ④ = E ② = B
⑤ = B ③ = G♯ ① = E

* Capo at 2nd fret

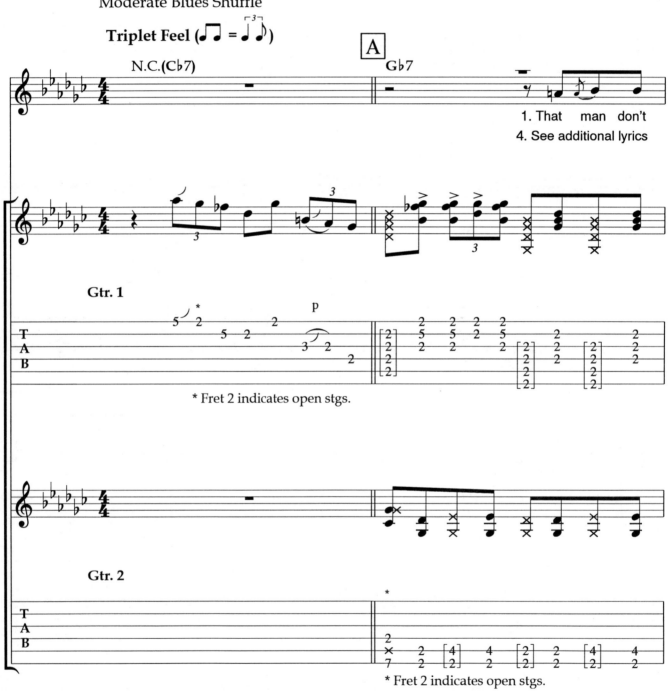

© 1989 LA CIENEGA MUSIC
This arranmgement © 1992 LA CIENEGA MUSIC
All Right Reserved

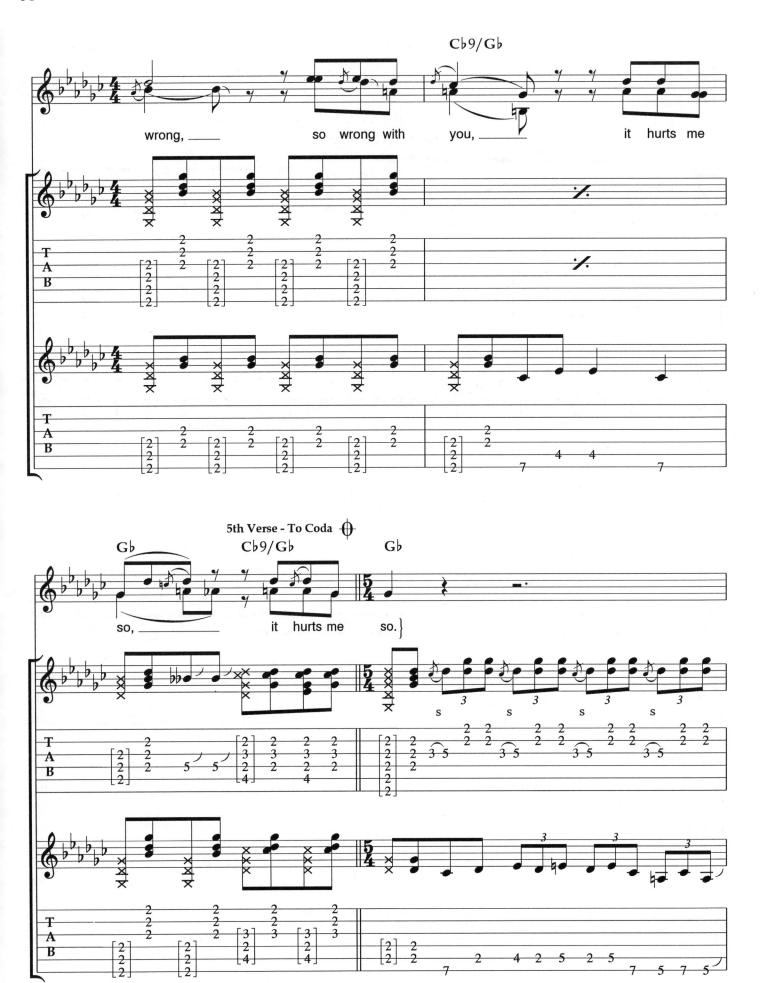

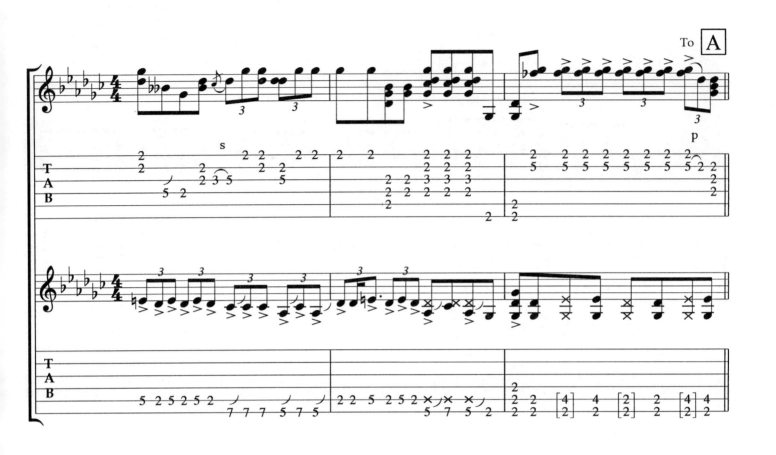
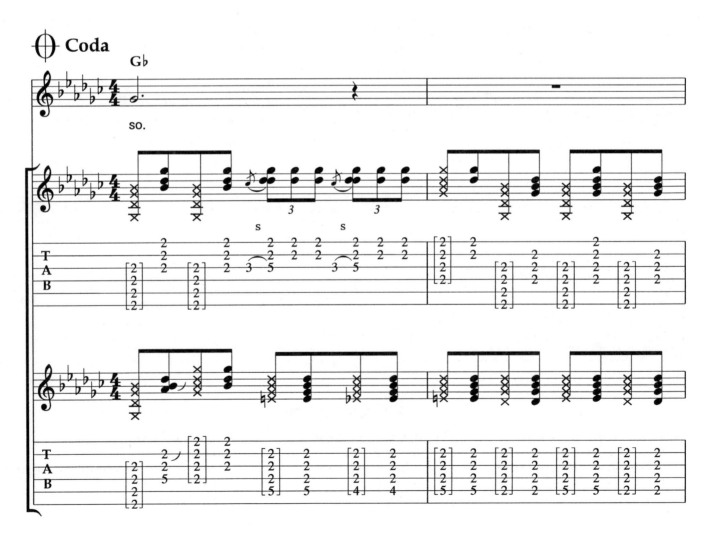

Additional Lyrics

3. You know you don't love him,
   You know you don't
   Go ahead an' leave me baby.
   Don't make me cry
   (To Chorus)

4. That man don't love you.
   He told me so.
   Only jivin' you, baby.
   Breaking up your home
   (To Chorus - 2x)

5. So long, baby.
   I've got to go,
   Because you don't love me now, darlin'.
   I know you don't.
   (To Chorus)

JOHN L'S HOUSE RENT BOOGIE

Transcribed Off The Album "John Lee Hooker : The Ultimate Collection (1948 - 1990)"

Words and Music by
John Lee Hooker and Bernard Besman

Guitar Tablature Transcription
by
Richard De Vinck

Open E Tuning:

⑥ = E ④ = E ② = B
⑤ = B ③ = G# ① = E

Capo at 2nd fret

Fast Blues

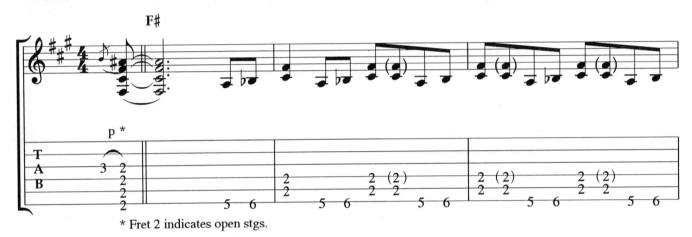

* Fret 2 indicates open stgs.

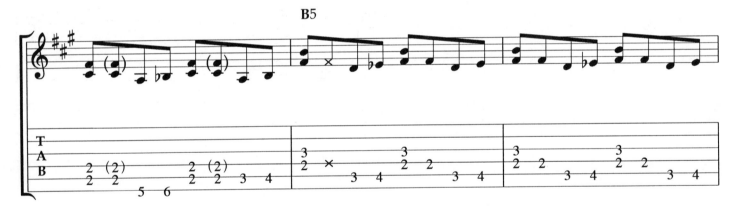

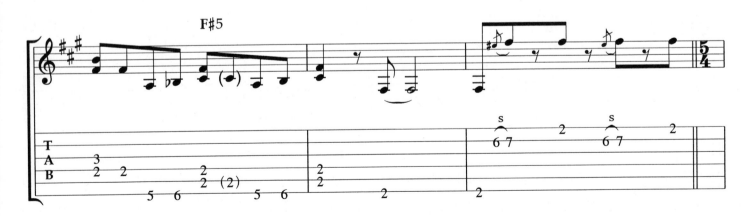

©1971, 1992 LA CIENEGA MUSIC
This arrangement © 1992 LA CIENEGA MUSIC
All rights Reserved

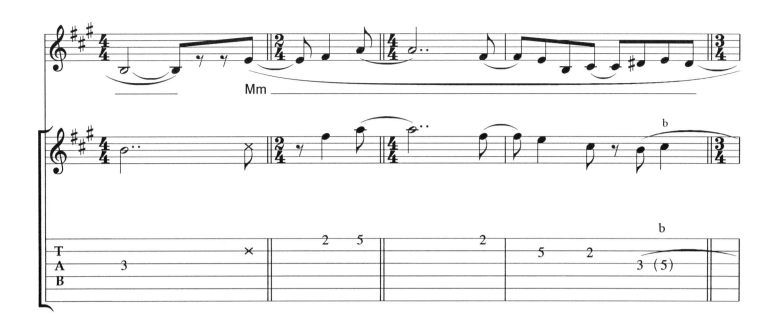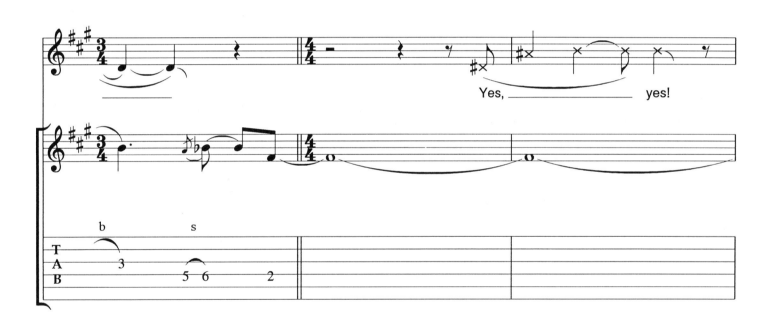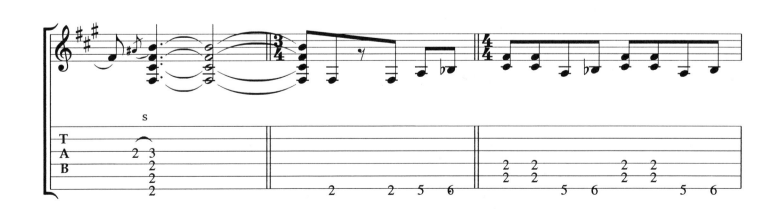

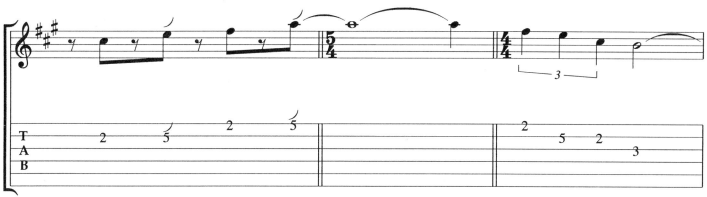
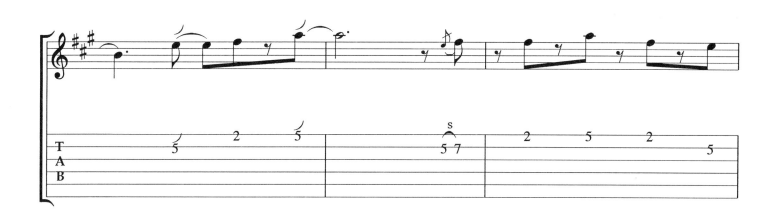

QUEEN BEE
Transcribed Off The Album "Half A Stranger"

Guitar Tablature Transcription
by
Richard De Vinck

Words and Music by
John Lee Hooker and Bernard Besman

Open E Tuning (Dropped A):

⑥ = E ④ = E ② = B
⑤ = A ③ = G# ① = E

Capo at 2nd fret

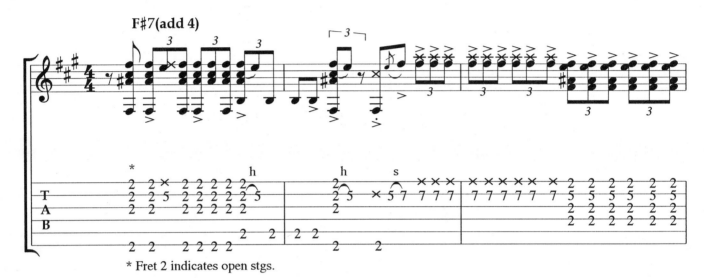

* Fret 2 indicates open stgs.

* Slightly ahead of the beat

© 1968 LA CIENEGA MUSIC
This arrangement © 1992 LA CIENEGA MUSIC
All rights Reserved

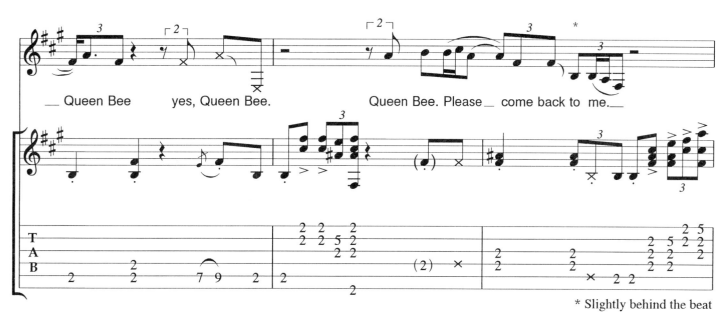

* Slightly behind the beat

115

Solo

Mm _____ sting-er long as my right arm. __

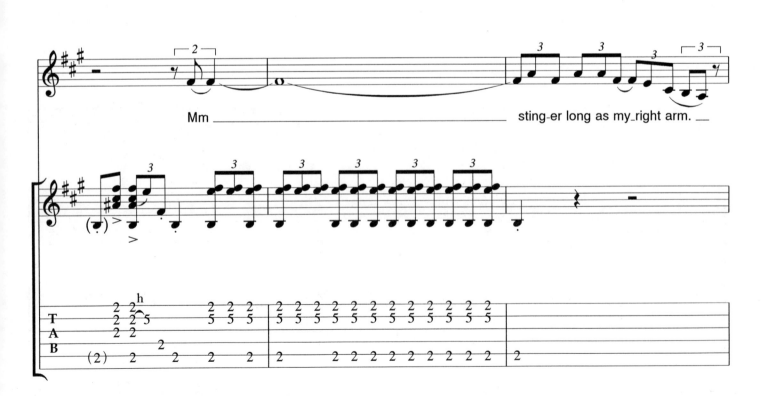

119

ROCK ME, MAMA
Transcribed Off The Album "Cold Chills"

Guitar Tablature Transcription
by
Richard De Vinck

Words and Music by
John Lee Hooker and Bernard Besman

Standard Tuning:
⑥ = E ④ = D ② = B
⑤ = A ③ = G ① = E

* Capo at 3rd fret

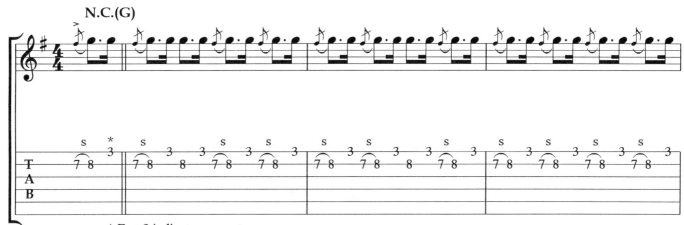

* Fret 3 indicates open stgs.

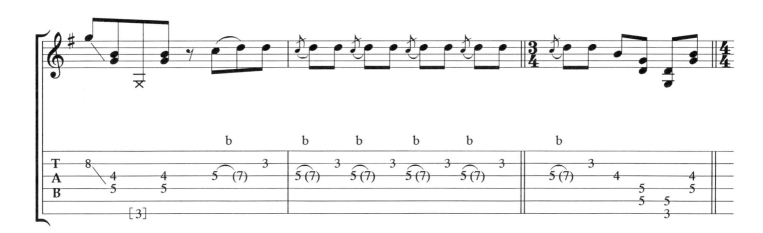

© 1952 and renewed 1980 LA CIENEGA MUSIC
This arrangement © 1992 LA CIENEGA MUSIC
All Rights Reserved

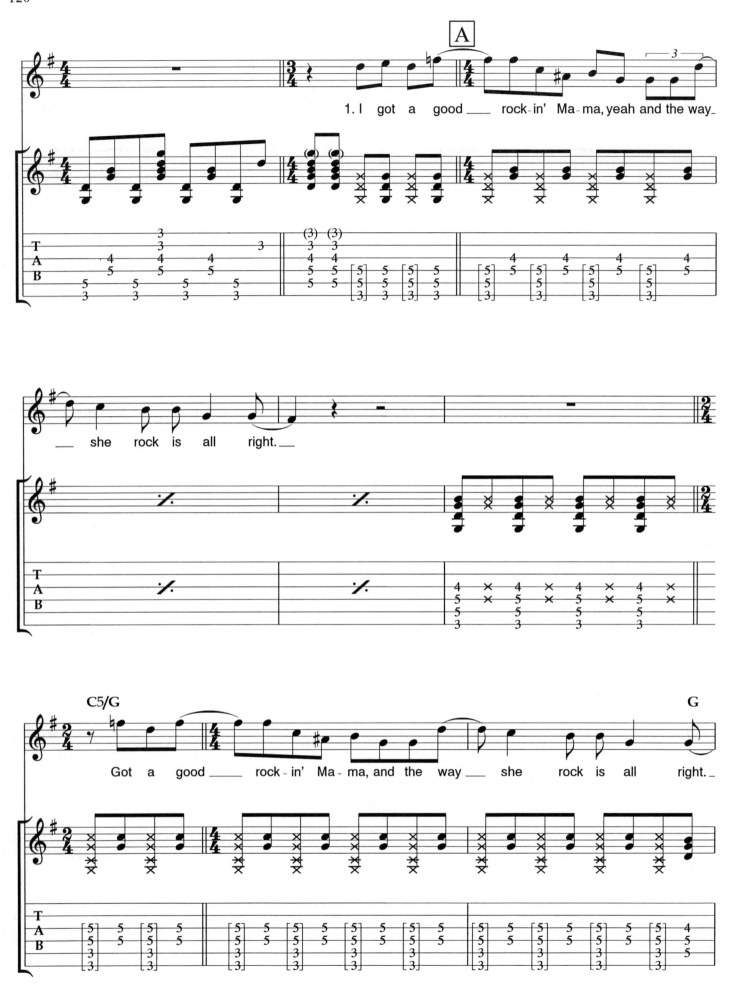

121

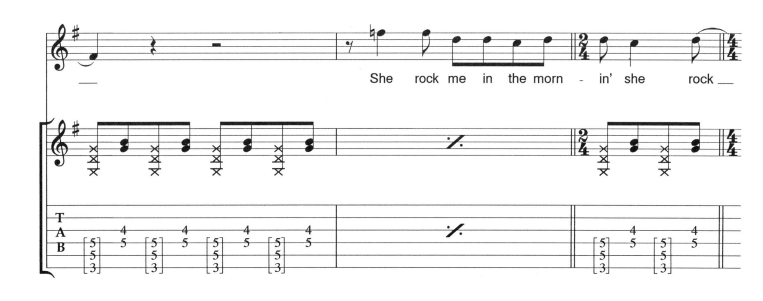

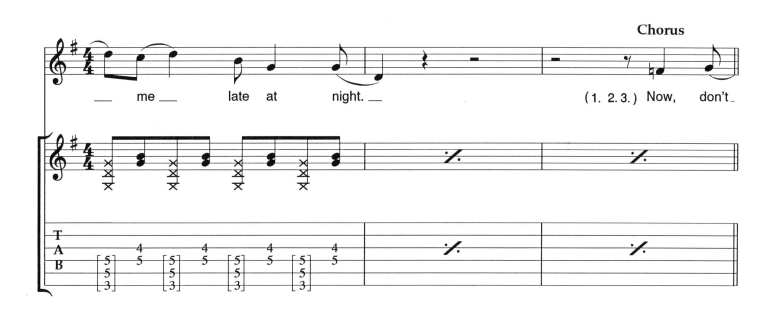

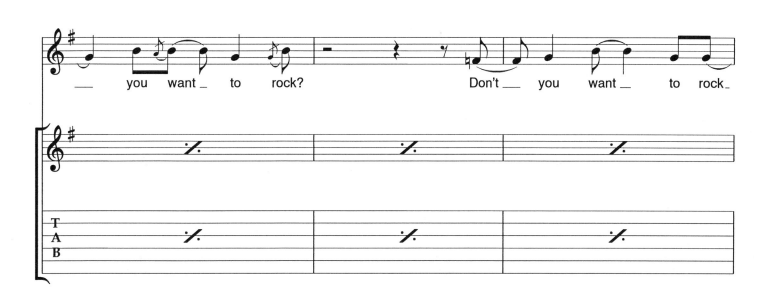

* During organ solos John Lee's guitar is barely audible. The pitches, rhythms, and frets are approximations.
** Repeats on 2nd organ solo only

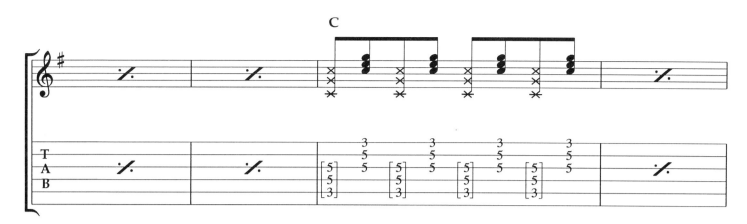

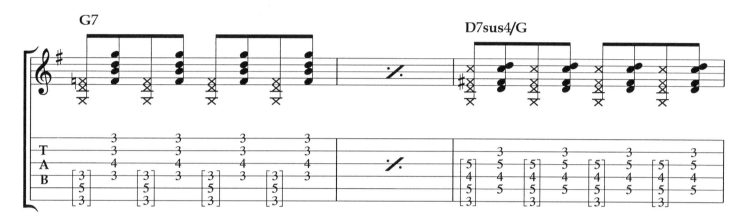

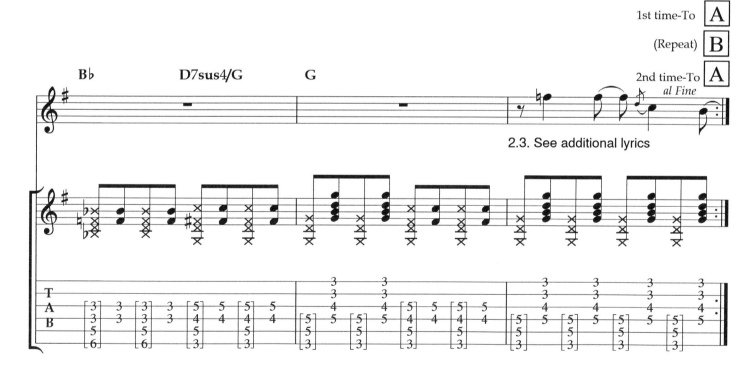

Additional Lyrics

2. We rocked last night and-a rocked the night before.
   We rocked last night and rocked the night before.
   Say, yes she rock me, rock me ev'ry night.
   (To chorus)

3. Don't need no steam heat, yo body keeps me warm.
   Don't need no steam heater, her body keeps me warm.
   She rocks me at midnight. She rock me till the break o'day.
   (To chorus)

SALLY MAE

Transcribed Off The Album "John Lee Hooker : The Ultimate Collection (1948 - 1990)"

Guitar Tablature Transcription
by
Richard De Vinck

Words and Music by
John Lee Hooker and Bernard Besman

Open A Tuning:

⑥ = E   ④ = E   ② = C#
⑤ = A   ③ = A   ① = E

Capo at 1st fret

Moderate Blues Shuffle

Triplet Feel (♪♪ = ♩♪)

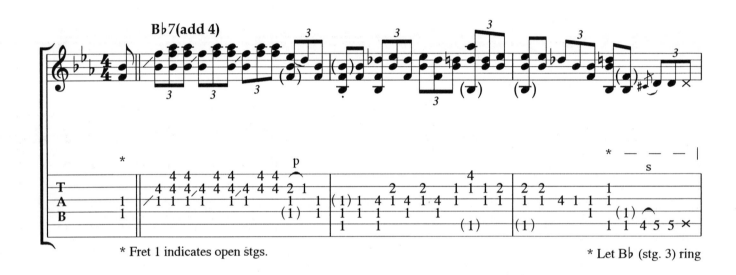

* Fret 1 indicates open stgs.   * Let B♭ (stg. 3) ring

© 1991 LA CIENEGA MUSIC
This arrangement © 1992 LA CIENEGA MUSIC
All Rights Reserved

125

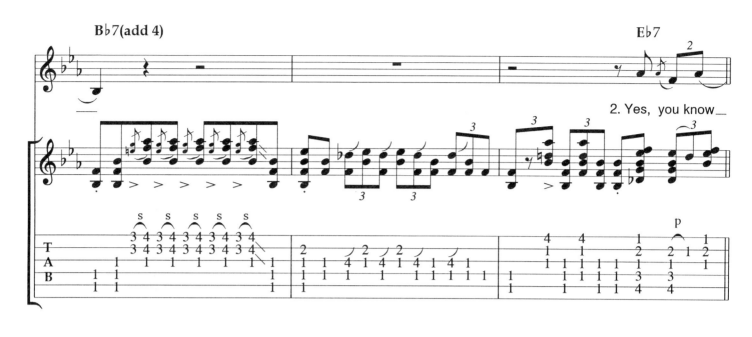

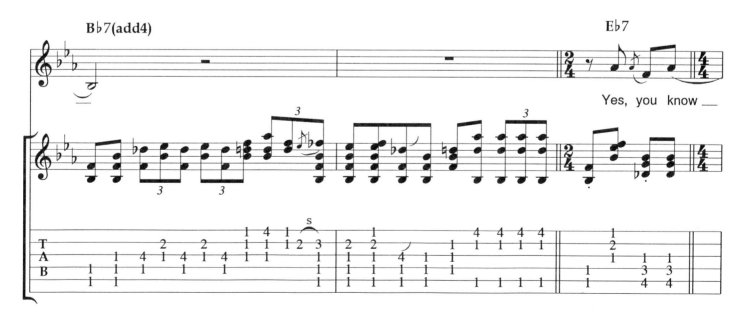

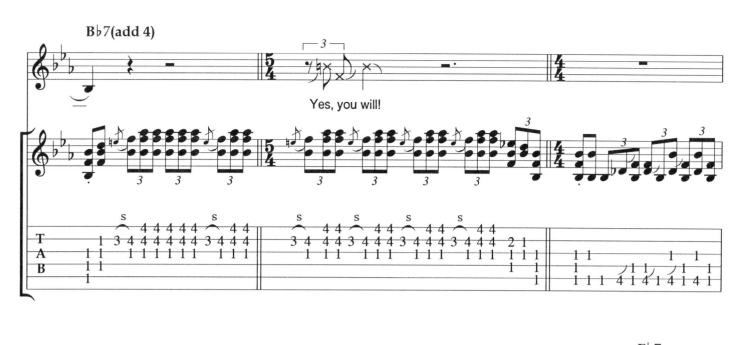

WEEPIN' WILLOW BOOGIE

Transcribed Off The Album "John Lee Hooker : The Ultimate Collection (1948 - 1990)"

Guitar Tablature Transcription by Richard De Vinck

Words and Music by John Lee Hooker and Bernard Besman

Open A Tuning:
⑥ = E ④ = E ② = C#
⑤ = A ③ = A ① = E

* Capo at 4th fret

* Fret 4 indicates open stgs.

© 1971 LA CIENEGA MUSIC
This arrangement © 1992 LA CIENEGA MUSIC
All rights Reserved

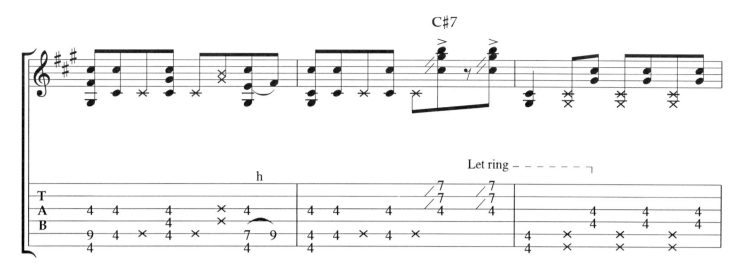
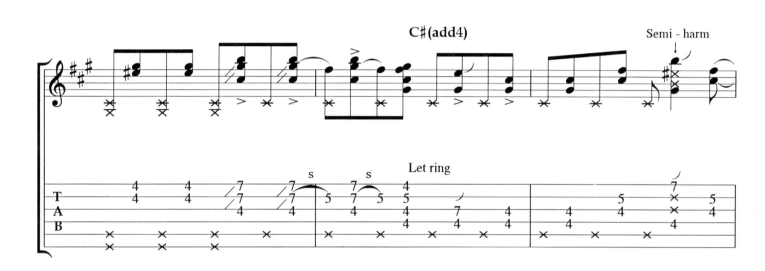

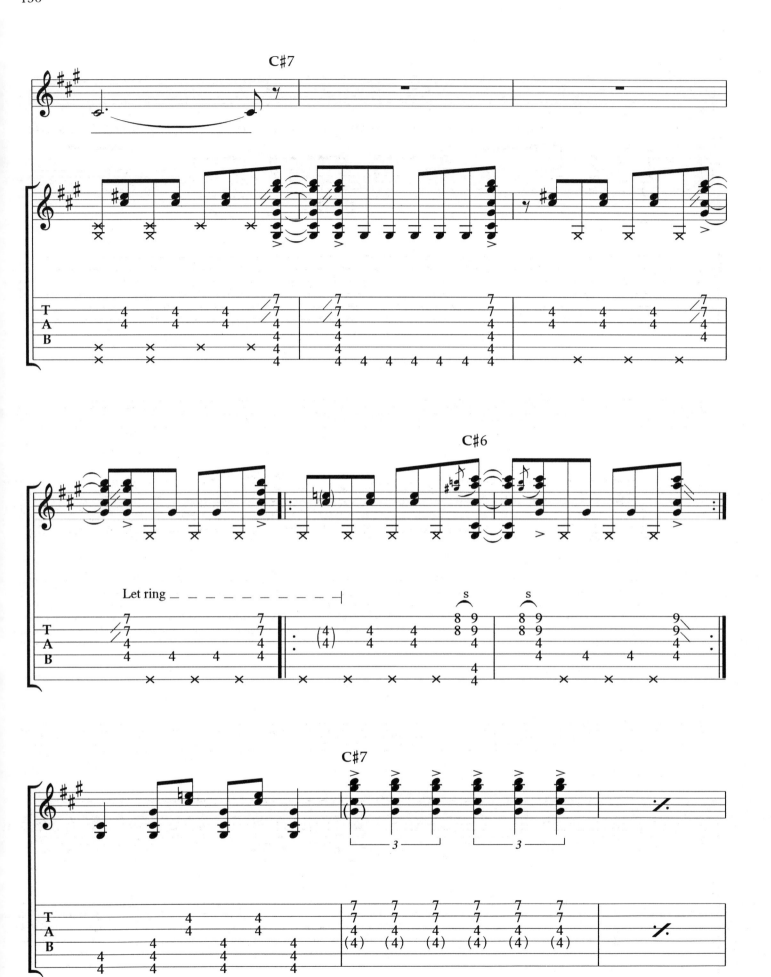

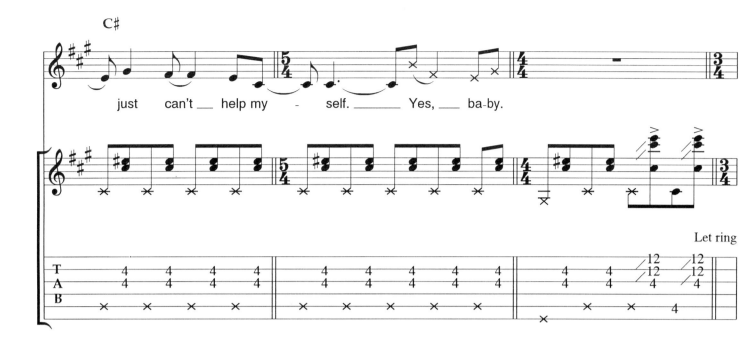
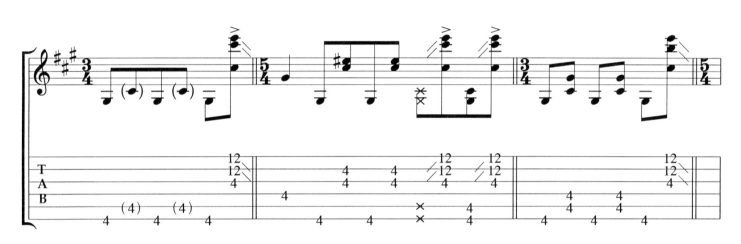
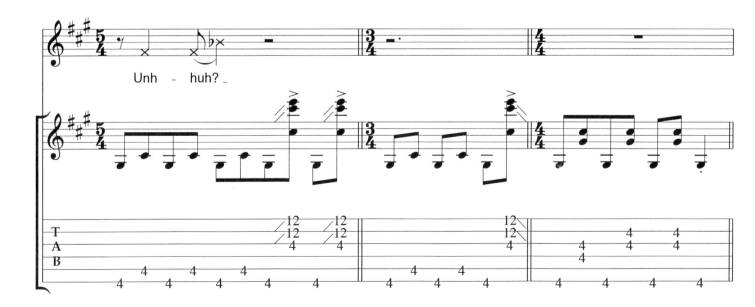

140

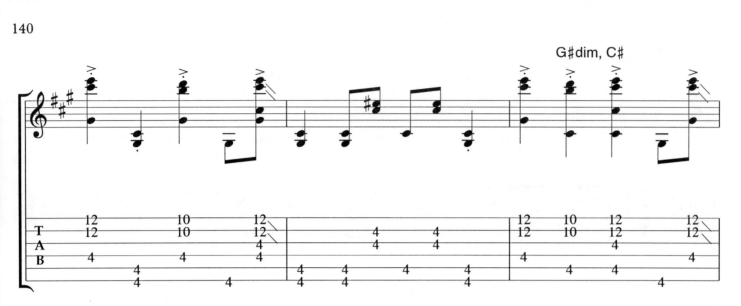

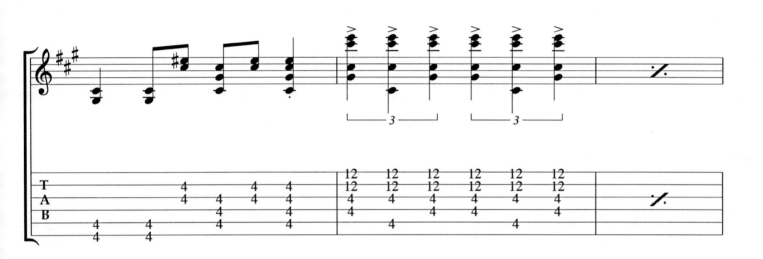

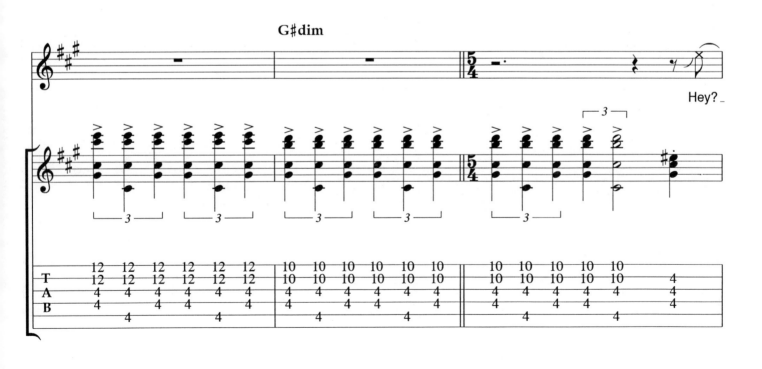

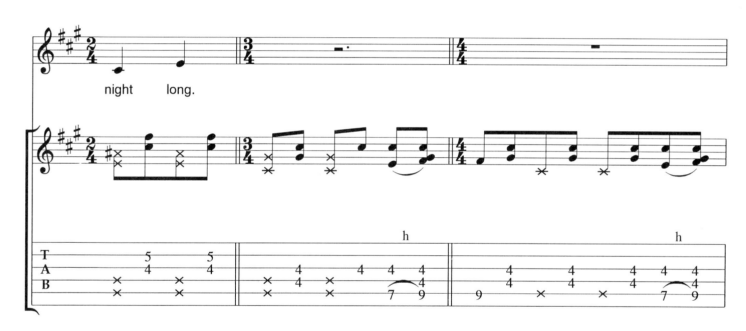

142

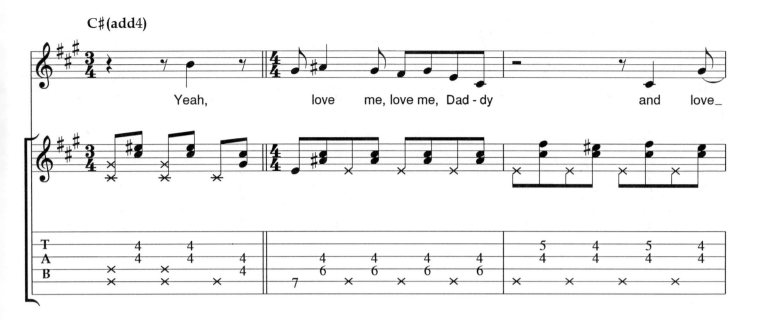
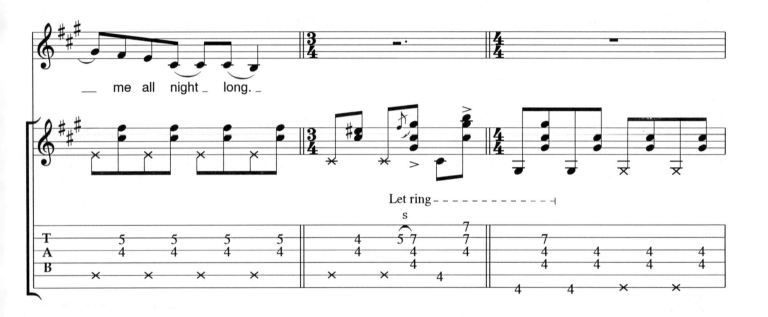
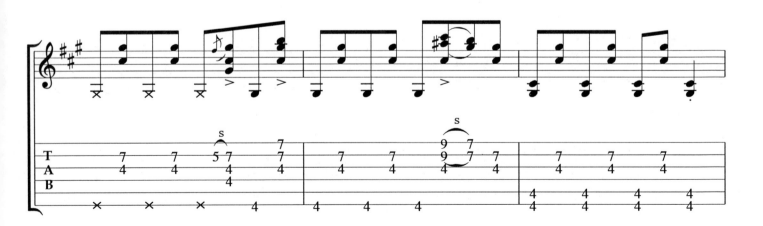

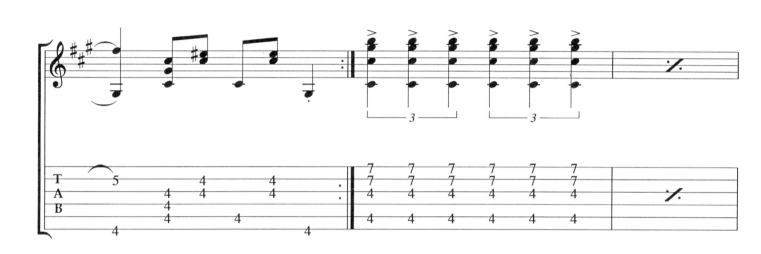

C#(add4)

'Cause your ba - by, _____ she need lov - in', lov -

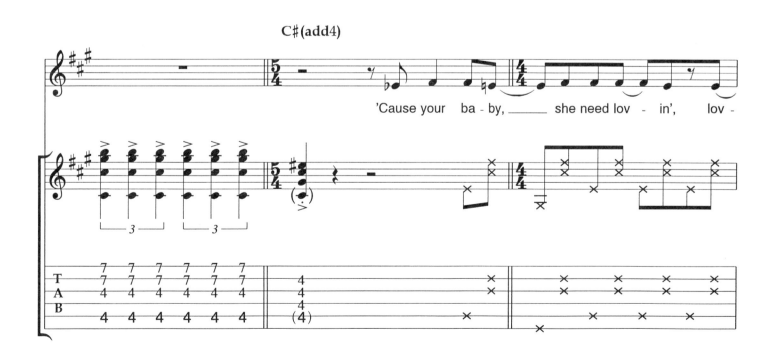

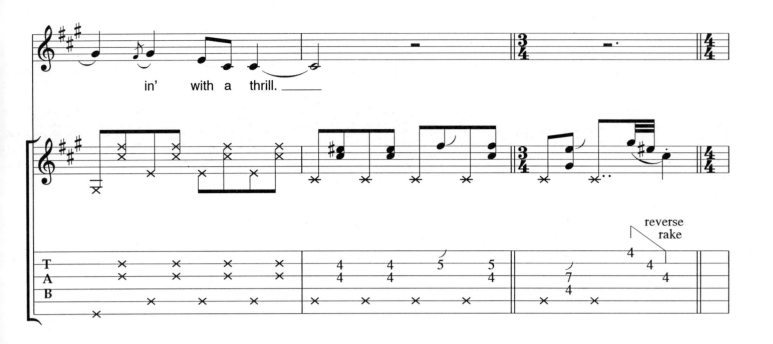
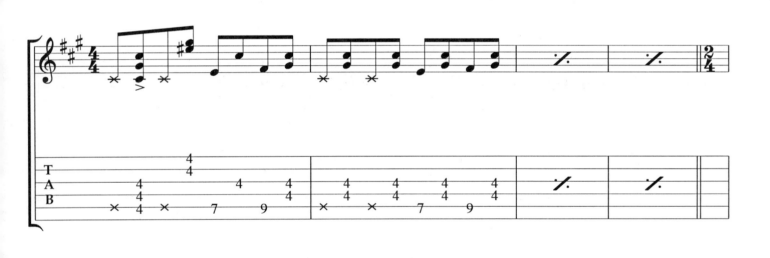
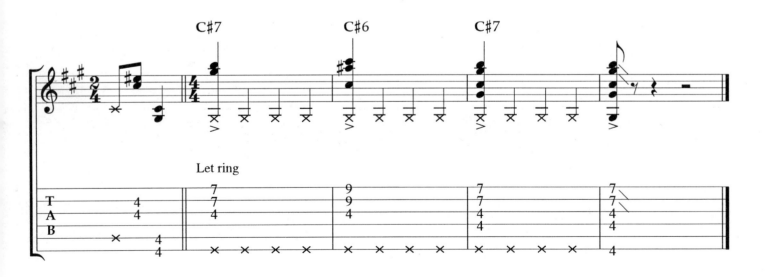

145

CRAWLIN' KING SNAKE

Transcribed Off The Album "John Lee Hooker : The Ultimate Collection (1948 - 1990)"

Guitar Tablature Transcription
by
Richard De Vinck

Words and Music by
John Lee Hooker and Bernard Besman

Open A Tuning:

⑥ = E ④ = E ② = C#
⑤ = A ③ = A ① = E

Slow Blues Shuffle

Triplet Feel

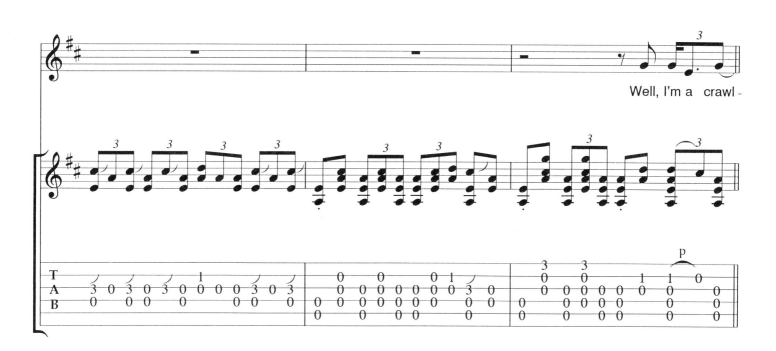

© 1968 LA CIENEGA MUSIC
This arrangement © 1994 LA CIENEGA MUSIC
All rights Reserved

147

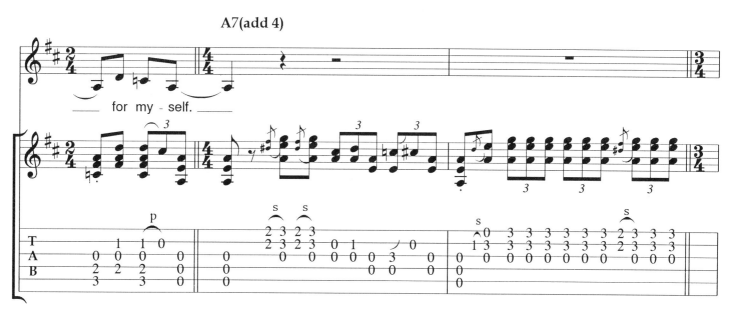

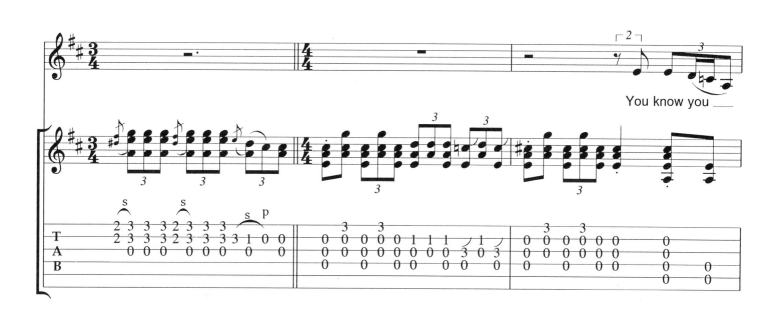

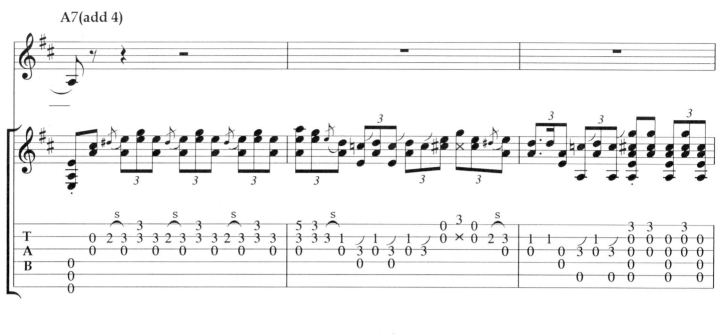

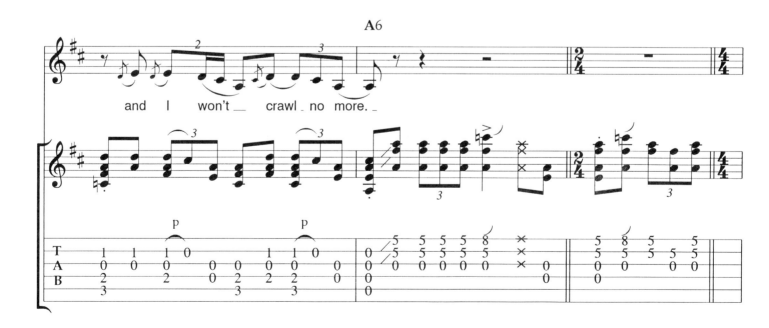

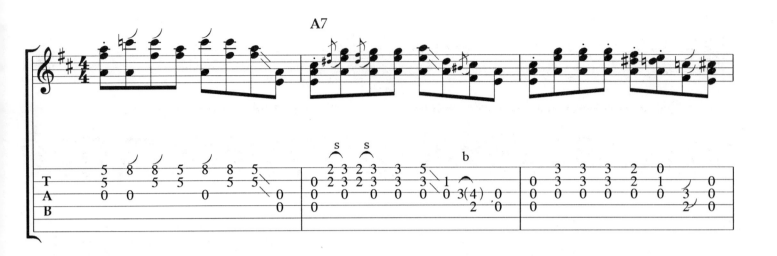
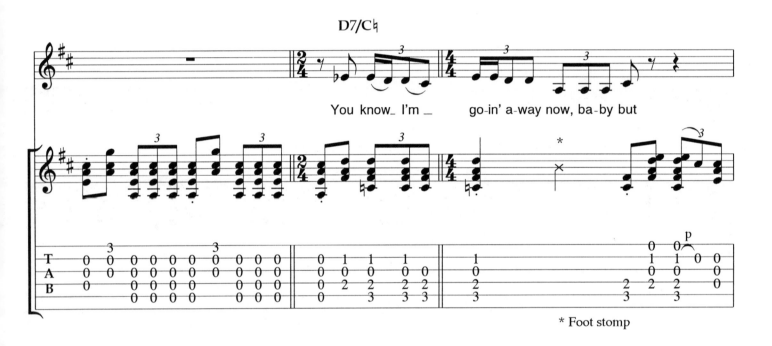

You know_ I'm _ go-in' a-way now, ba-by but

*Foot stomp

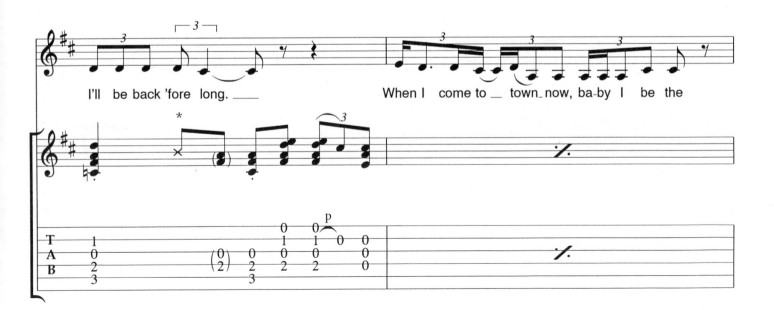

I'll be back 'fore long. ___ When I come to _ town_ now, ba-by I be the

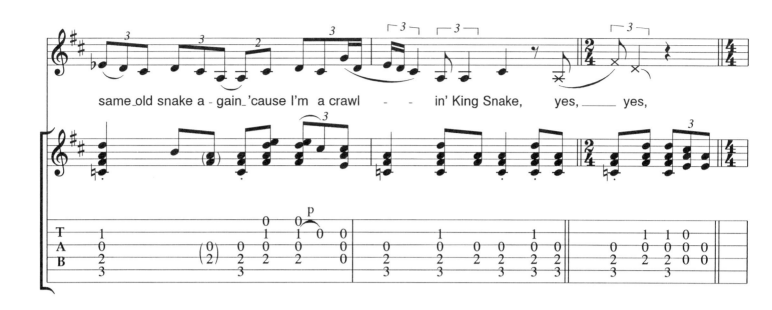
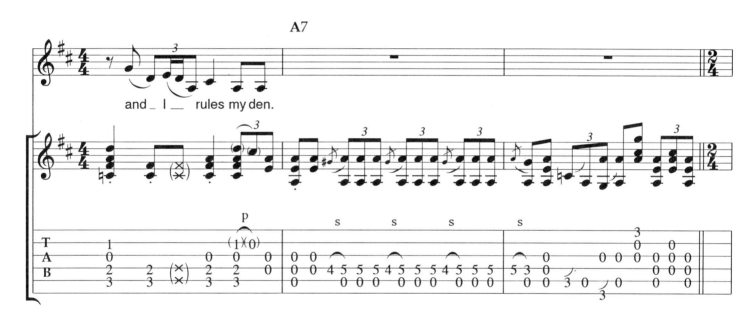

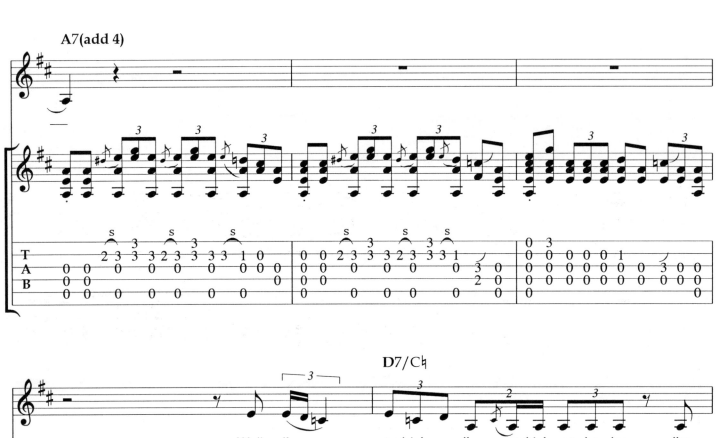
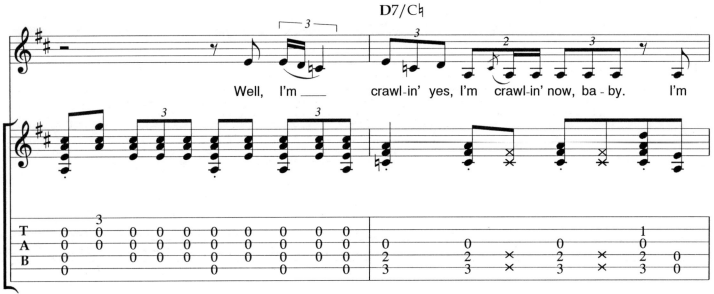
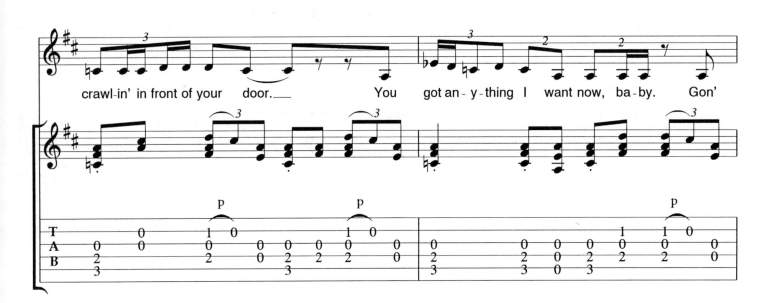

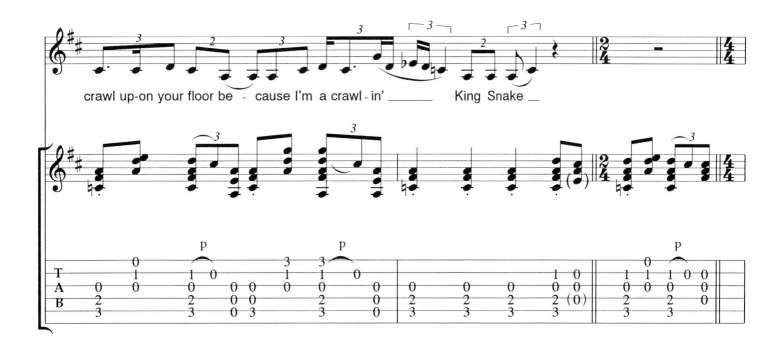
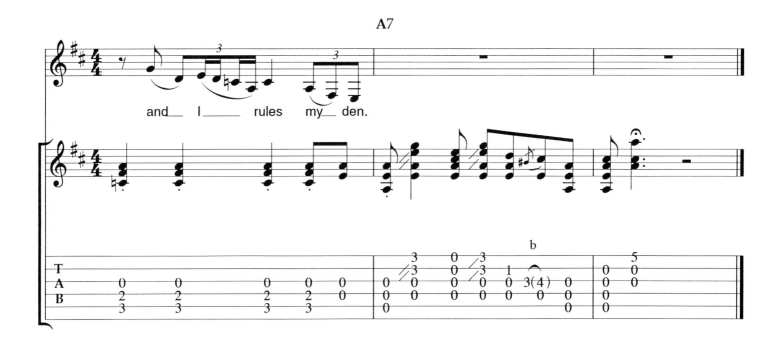

THIS IS 19 AND 52, BABE
(Turn Over A New Leaf)
Transcribed Off The Album "John Lee Hooker's 40th Anniversary Album"

Guitar Tablature Transcription
by
Richard De Vinck

Words and Music by
John Lee Hooker and Bernard Besman

Open A Tuning:
⑥ = E ④ = E ② = C#
⑤ = A ③ = A ① = E

* Capo at 3rd fret

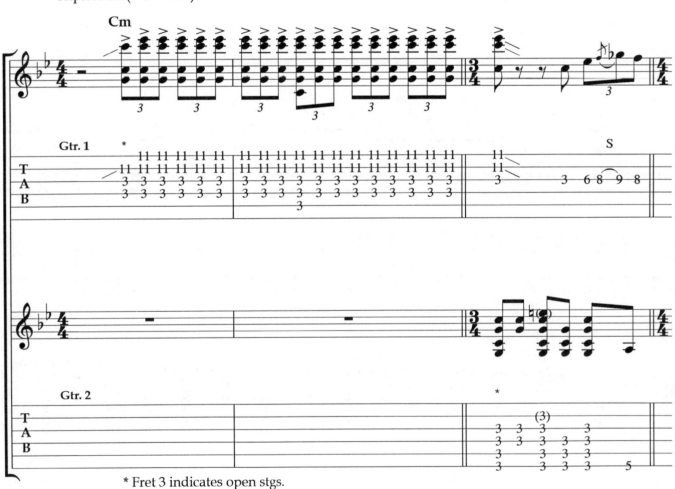

* Fret 3 indicates open stgs.

© 1989 LA CIENEGA MUSIC
This arrangement © 1994 LA CIENEGA MUSIC
All Rights Reserved

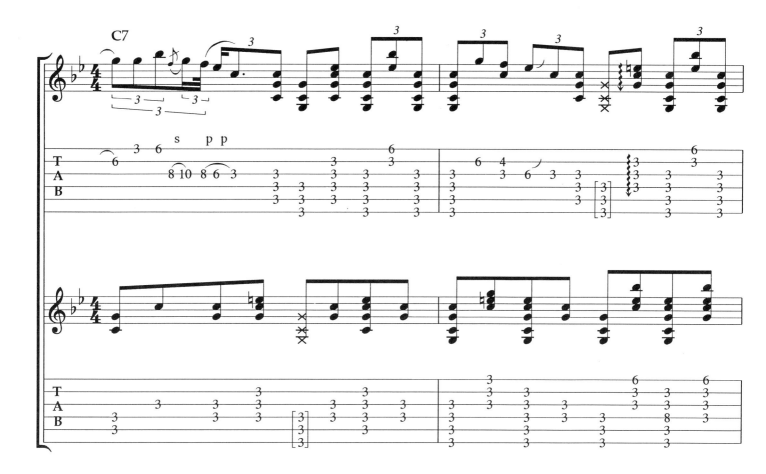

158

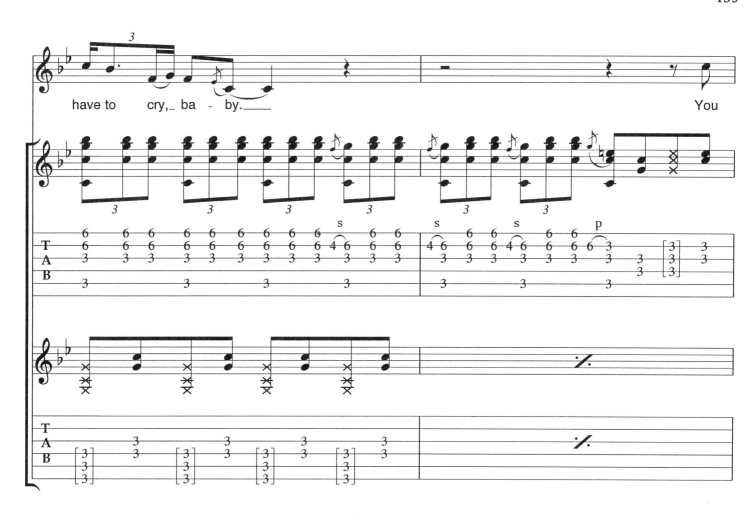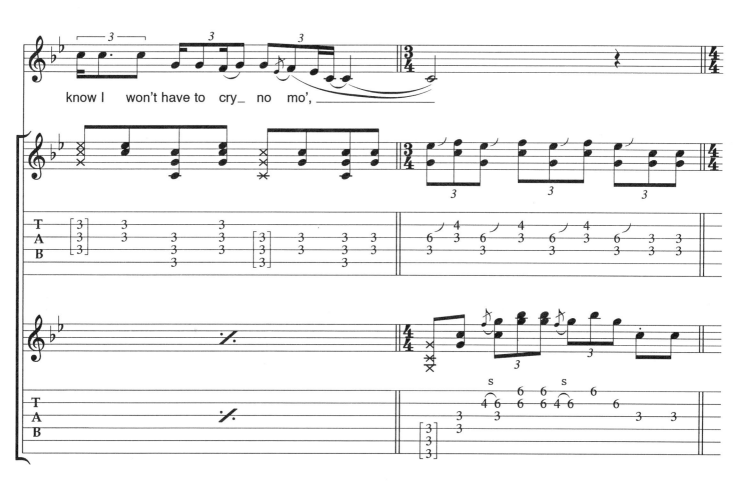

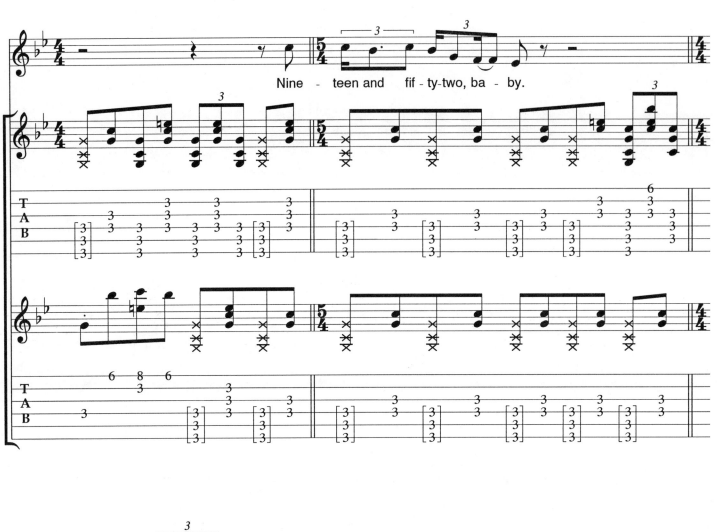
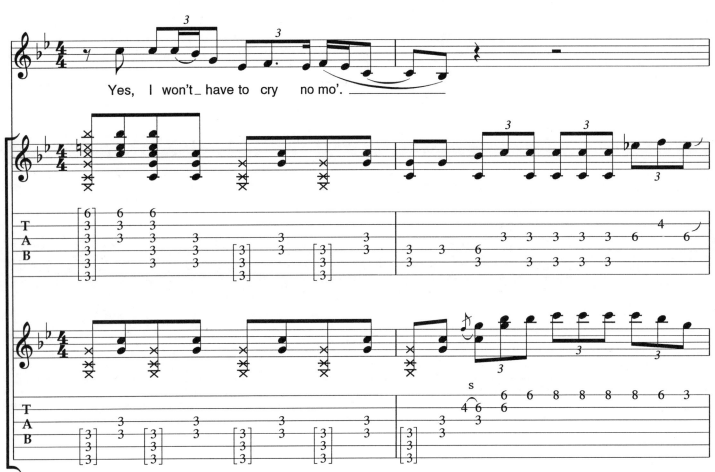

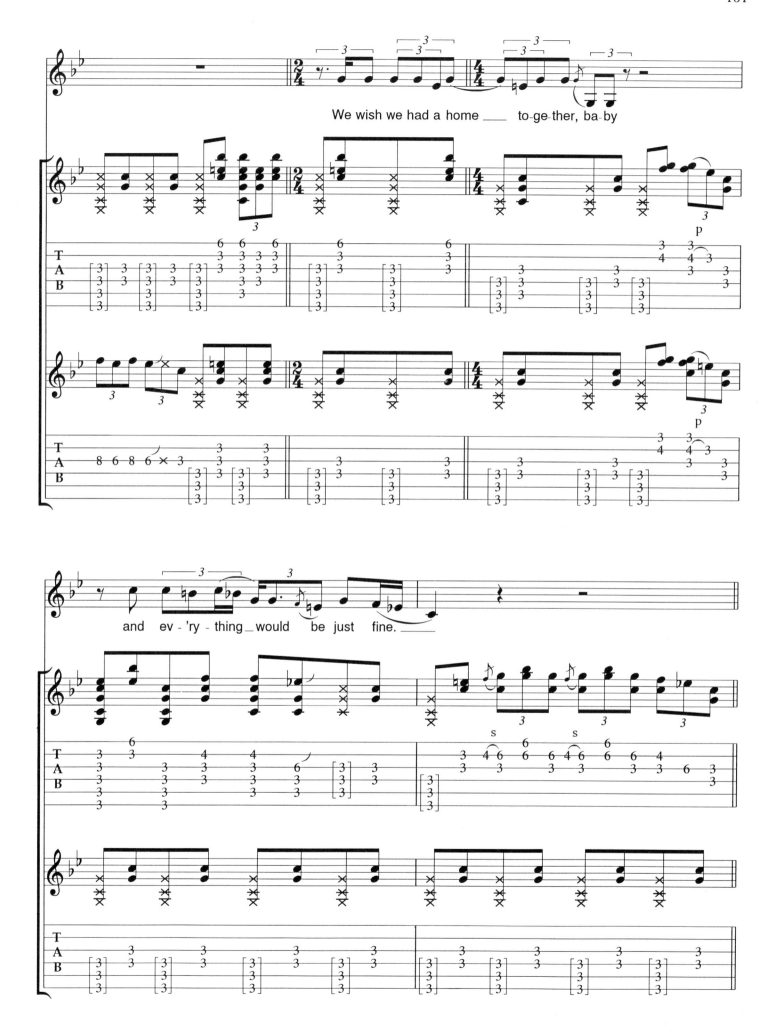

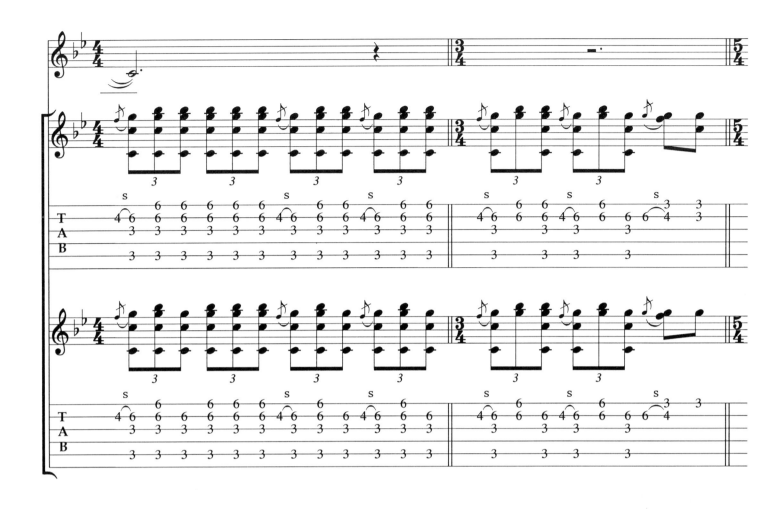
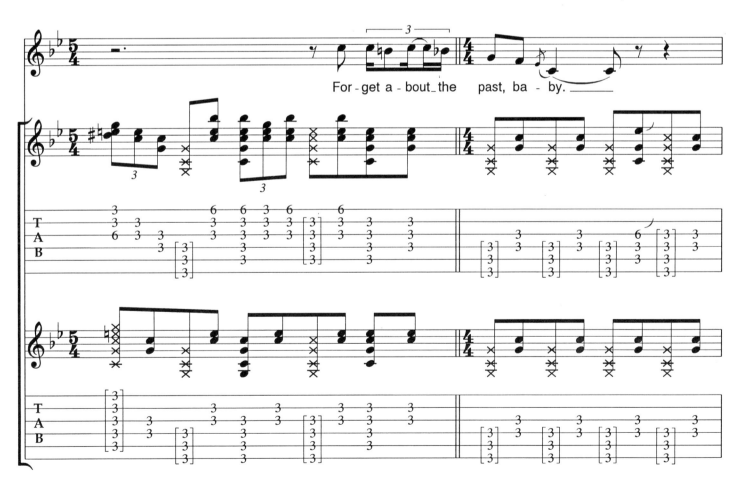

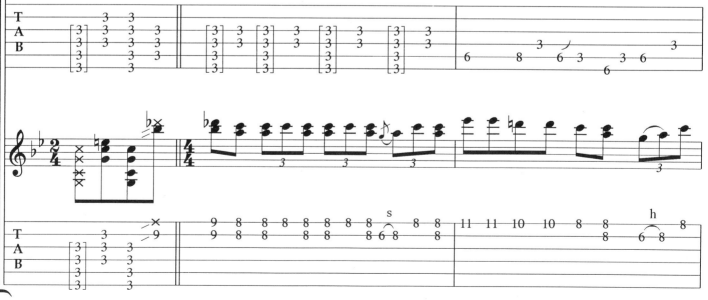

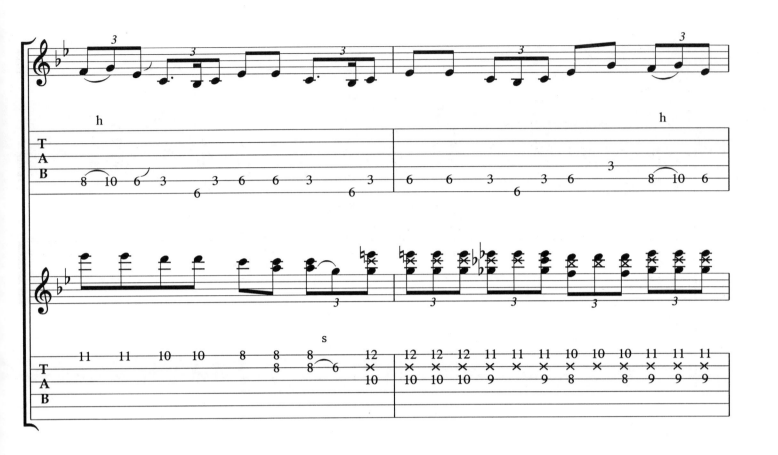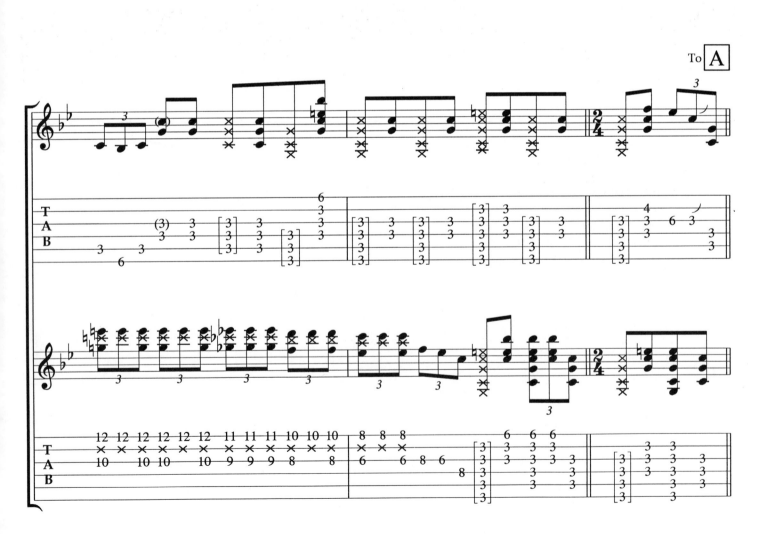

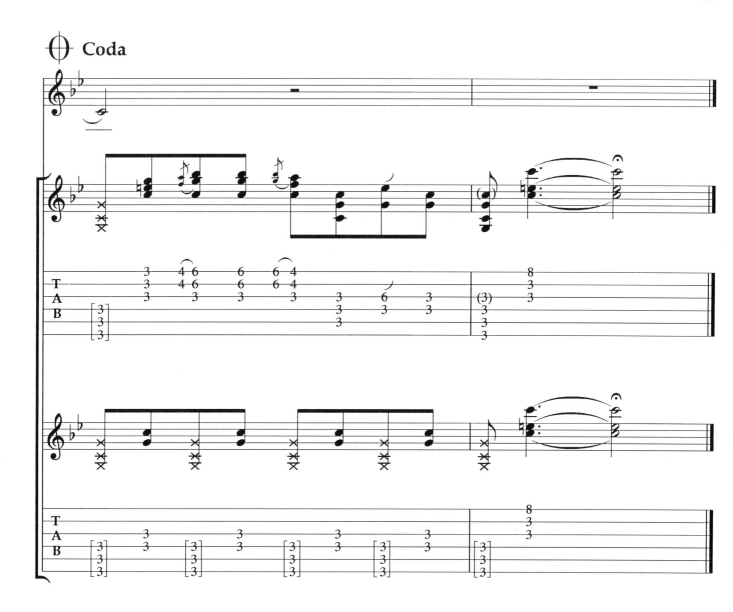

Additional Lyrics

4. You know the future may bring, bring baby.
   It may bring happiness in our home.
   Yeah, the future, baby
   It may bring happiness in our home
   This is 19 and 52 babe.
   Gonna turn over a brand new leaf.

DO MY BABY THINK OF ME?

Transcribed Off The Album "John Lee Hookers 40th Anniversary Album"

Guitar Tablature Transcription
by
Richard De Vinck

Standard Tuning:
⑥ = E ④ = D ② = B
⑤ = A ③ = G ① = E

Words and Music by
John Lee Hooker and Bernard Besman

* Throughout Intro-rest heel of R.H. on stgs. ⑥ through ② at bridge to slightly mute those stgs. letting stg. ① ring.

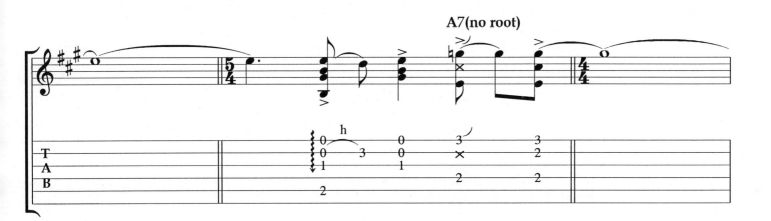

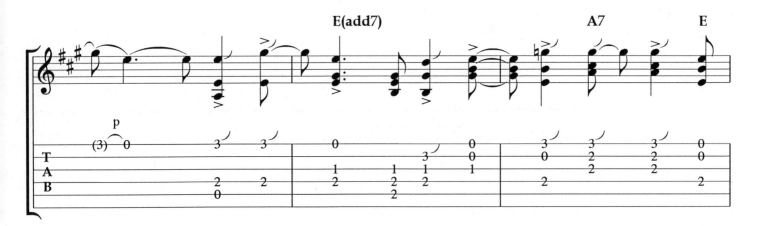

© 1970 LA CIENEGA MUSIC
This arrangement © 1994 LA CIENEGA MUSIC
All Rights Reserved

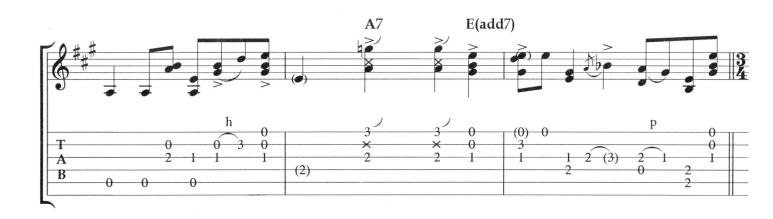
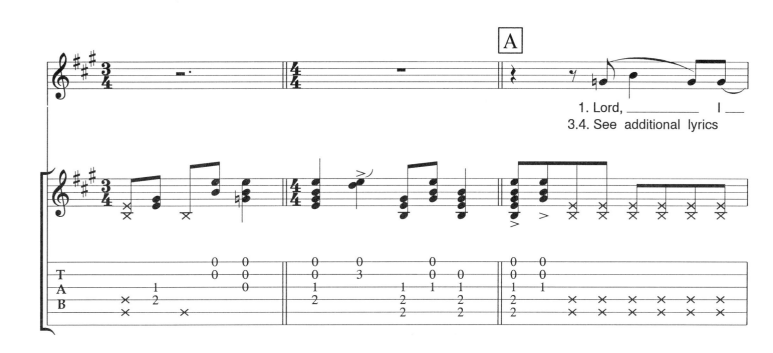
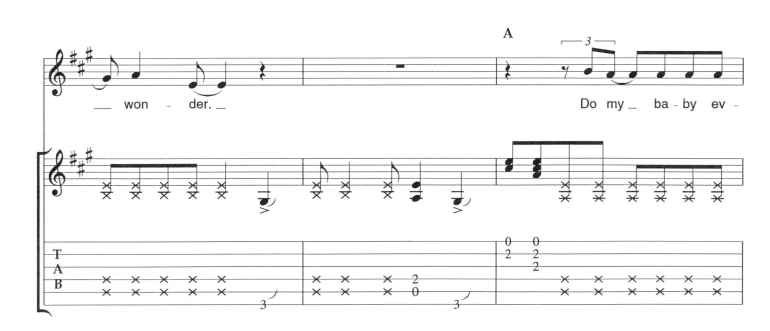

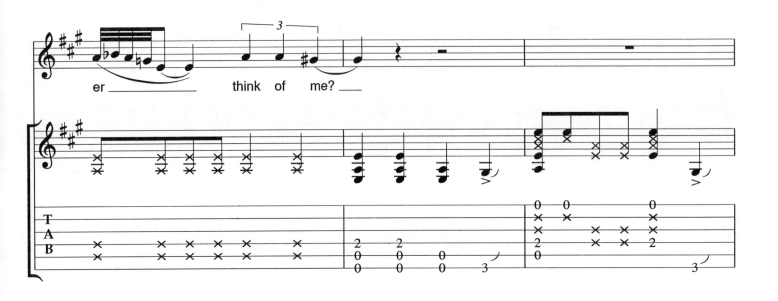
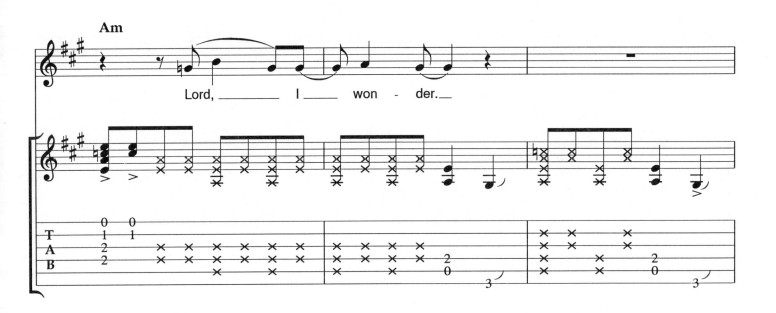
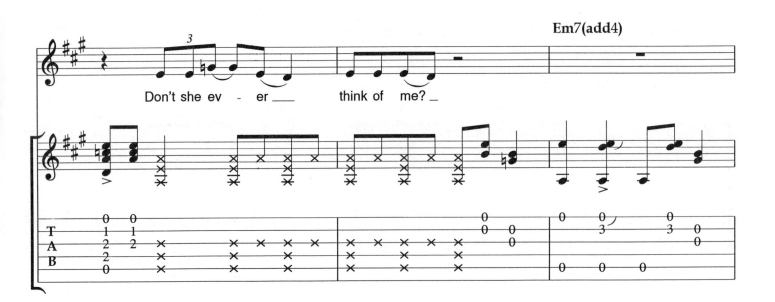

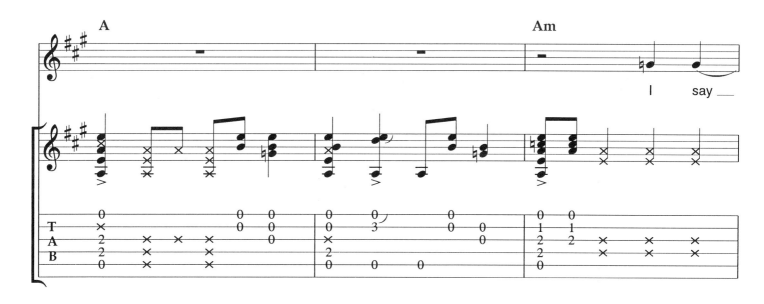
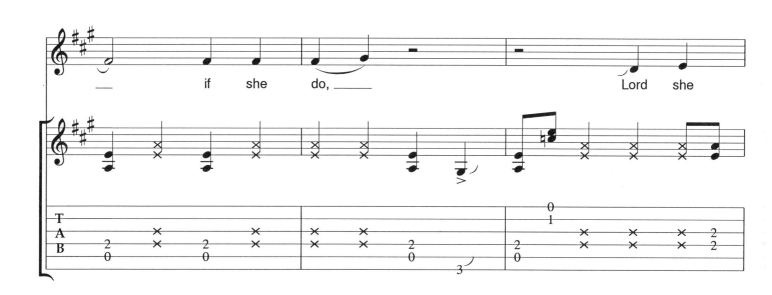
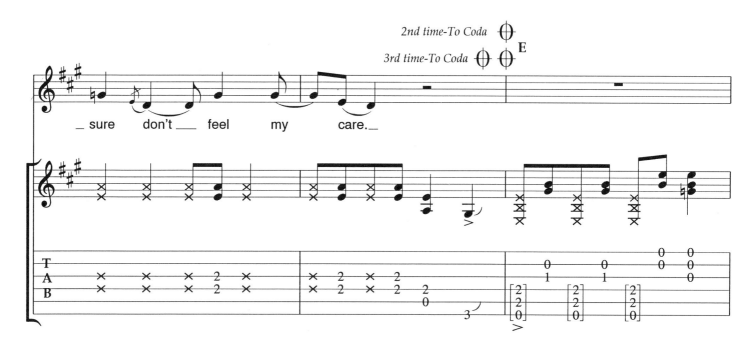

173

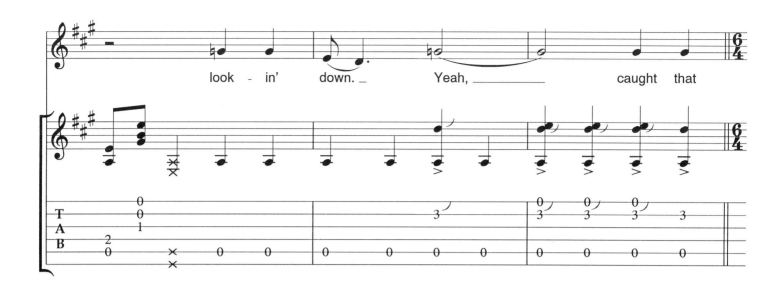

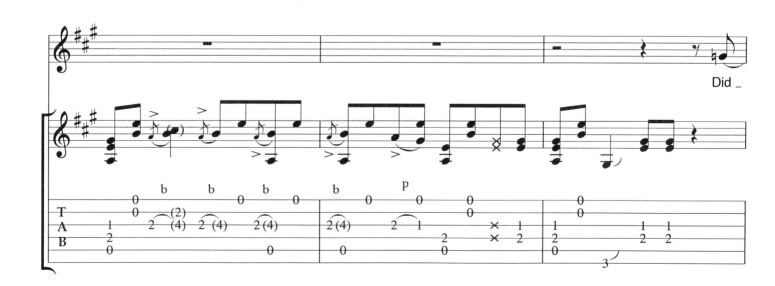

* Strike gtr. w / R.H. thumb

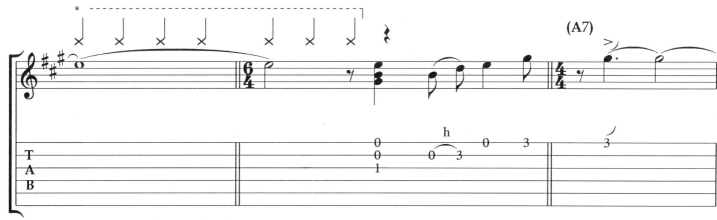

*Slap gtr. w / R.H. thumb

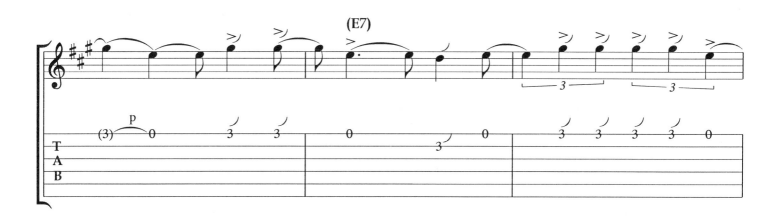

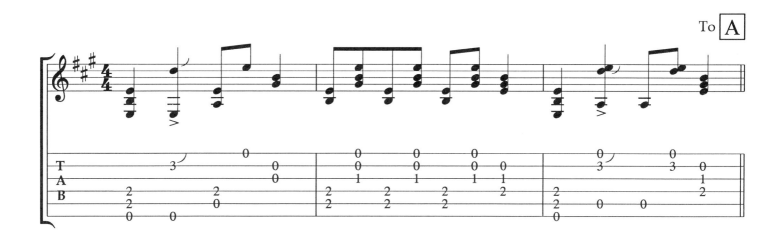

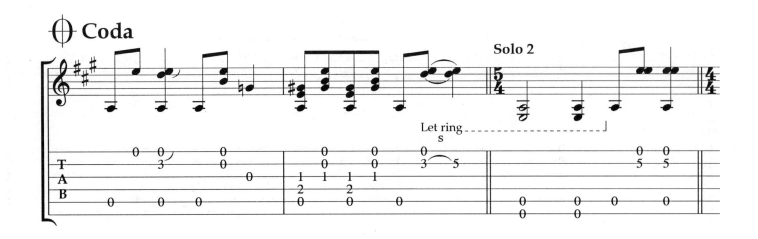
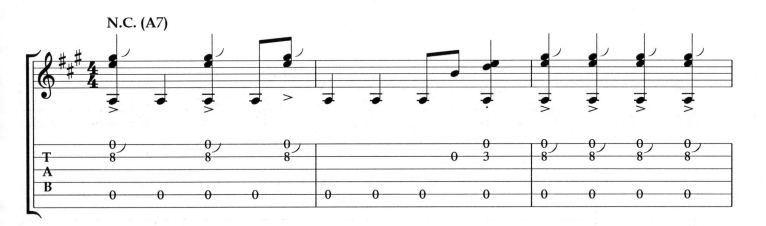
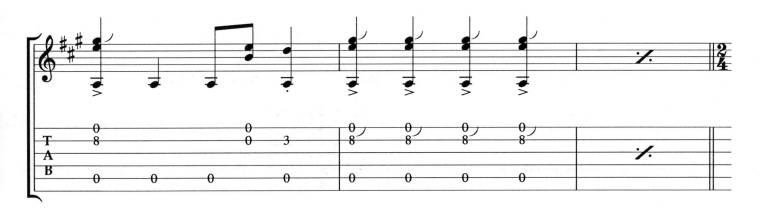
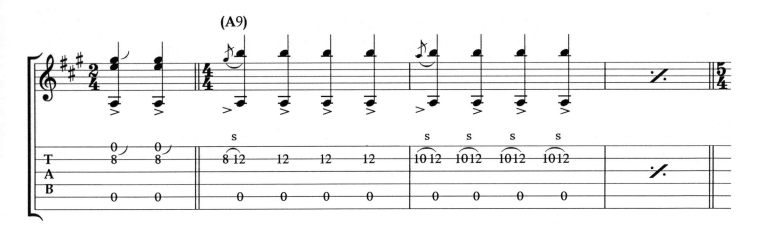

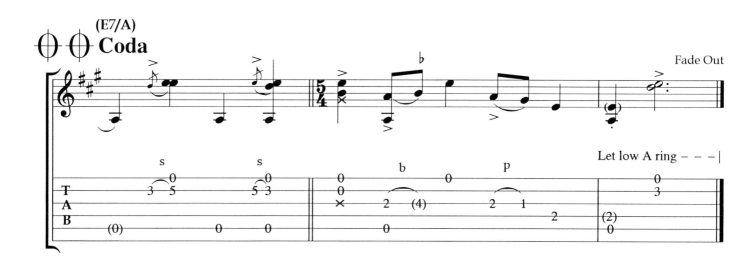

Additional Lyrics

3. Lord, I ain't got no
   Special Rider here. (No I ain't)
   Lord, I ain't got no
   Special Rider here.
   I'm gonna leave in the morn-in'
   'Cause I don't feel welcome here.

4. Lord, I wonder
   Do my baby ever think of me? (Yes, yes, yeah)
   Lord, I wonder
   Don't she ever think of me?
   'Cause I'm gonna leave, leave
   'Cause I don't feel welcome here.

HOBO BLUES

Transcribed Off The Album "John Lee Hooker : The Ultimate Collection (1948 - 1990)"

Guitar Tablature Transcription
by
Richard De Vinck

Words and Music by
John Lee Hooker and Bernard Besman

Open A Tuning:

⑥ = E ④ = E ② = C#
⑤ = A ③ = A ① = E

Moderate Blues Shuffle

Triplet Feel

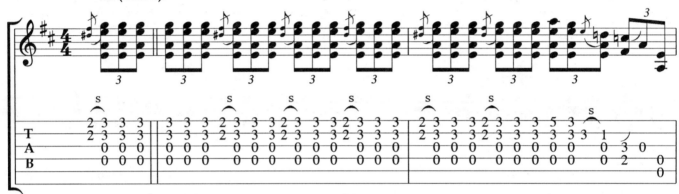

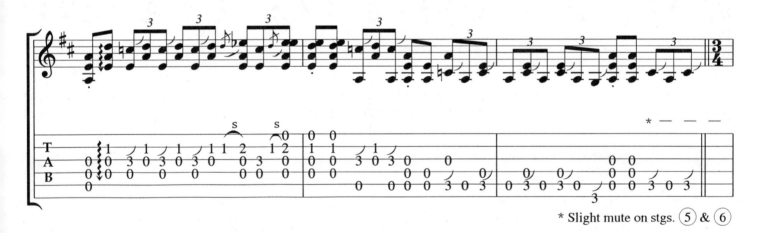

* Slight mute on stgs. ⑤ & ⑥

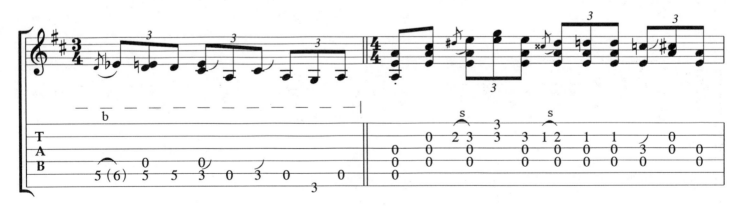

© 1968 LA CIENEGA MUSIC
This arrangement © 1994 LA CIENEGA MUSIC
All rights Reserved

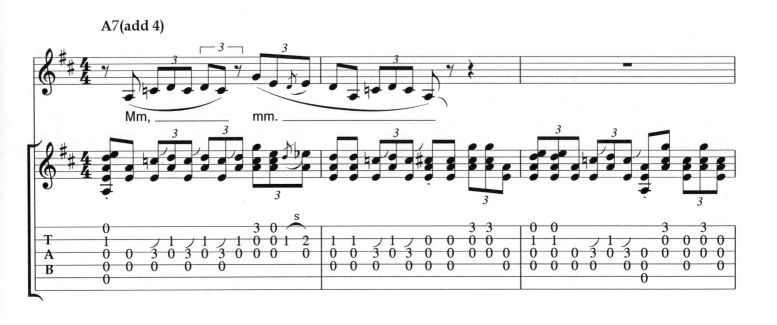
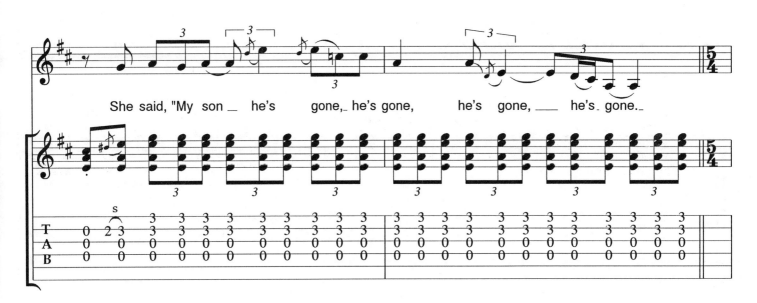

183

You know I love my dear ____ old moth-

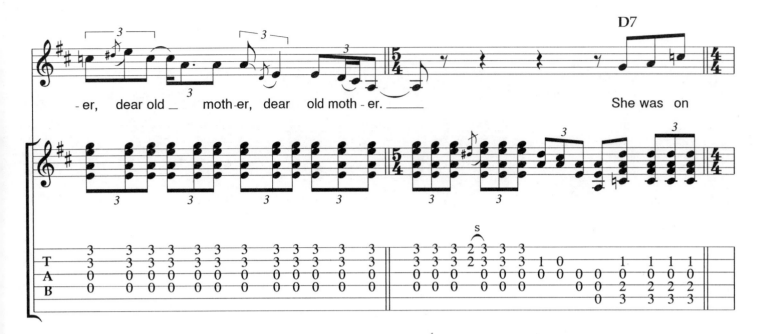

-er, dear old ____ moth-er, dear old moth-er. _____ She was on

BLUES TABLATURE GUITAR TRANSCRIPTIONS
The Vital Blues Guitar Series NEW!

BUDDY GUY - VITAL BLUES GUITAR - Transcribed by Richard DeVinck
Note-For-Note Tablature transcriptions plus Standard Music Notation. Songs from eight great albums plus bio & many photos. Complete contents: Buddy's Groove • Five Long Years • I Can't Quit The Blues • I Could Cry • I Had A Dream Last Night • I Smell A Rat • A Man And The Blues • Messin' With The Kid • Mustang Sally • She Suits Me To A T • She's Out There Somewhere • Stick Around • There's Something On Your Mind • Worry, Worry, Worry.
Catalog No. 07-4032 $19.95

HOT BLUES GUITAR #1 - Transcribed by Roy Zimmerman
Note-For-Note Tablature transcriptions plus Standard Music Notation. Songs by Muddy Waters, The Allman Brothers, Willie Dixon, George Thorogood, Little Walter, Buddy Buy, Slim Harpo, Keith Richards, James Burton, Scotty Moore & others. Complete contents: Baby, Let's Play House • Call It Stormy Monday • Can't Stop Lovin' • Evil Ways • Five Long Years • Gambler's Blues • Got My Mojo Working • Harlem Nocturne • I'm A King Bee • I'm Your Hoochie Coochie Man • Last Affair •Mean And Evil • The Midnight Special • My Babe • Night Life • Rock Me Baby • The Seventh Son • Shake Your Hips • Sunnyland • The Thrill Is Gone • Three O'clock Blues • Trouble, No More.
Catalog No. 07-4028 $19.95

HOT BLUES GUITAR #2 - Transcribed by Billy Simms
Note-For-Note Tablature transcriptions plus Standard Music Notation. Songs by Lowell Fulsom, Johnny "Guitar" Watson, Earl Hooker, Albert Collins, Robert Cray, Freddie King, The Fabulous Thunderbirds, Johnny Copeland, Howlin' Wolf & others. Complete contents: Ain't No Sunshine • Back Door Friend • Bad Luck Soul • Black Cat Bone • Camp Washington Chili • Dog Me Around • The Freeze • Get Out Of Here • Hot Little Mama • The Huckle Buck • Pressure Cooker • Standing At The Crossroads • Talkin' Woman • Three Hours Past Midnight • Tramp • Tuff Enuff • Work Song • Worried About My Baby.
Catalog No. 07-4039 $19.95

T-BONE WALKER - VITAL BLUES GUITAR - Transcribed by Richard DeVinck
Note-For-Note Tablature transcriptions plus Standard Music Notation. The best from the father of the electric blues guitar. Complete contents: Call It Stormy Monday • Glamour Girl • Good Boy • Got To Cross The Deep Blue Sea • I Got A Break Baby • Left Home When I Was A Kid • Louisiana Bayou Drive • Mean Old World • My Patience Keeps Running Out • Natural Ball • A Slave Like Me • Treat Your Daddy Well • Why Won't My Baby Treat Me Right? • You Don't Know What You're Doing.
Catalog No. 07-4033 $19.95

LIGHTNIN' HOPKINS - VITAL BLUES GUITAR - Transcribed by Richard DeVinck
Note-For-Note Tablature transcriptions plus Standard Music Notation. Great Texas Blues Guitar. Complete contents: Appetite Blues • Back Door Friend • Black Cat • Gambler's Blues • House Upon The Hill • I'm Comin' Home • Jake Head Boogie •Love Me This Mornin' • Mistreated Blues • Move On Out (Pt.2) • One Kind Favor • Santa Fe Blues • Someday, Baby • You're Too Fast.
Catalog No. 07-4031 $19.95

B.B. KING - VITAL BLUES GUITAR - Transcribed by Richard DeVinck
Note-For-Note Tablature transcriptions plus Standard Music Notation. There are other B.B. King books but none are as accurate and none have the song selection of this fine, fine book. Complete contents: Baby Get Lost • Darlin' You Know I Love You • Guess Who • It's Just A Matter Of Time • Night Life • Rock Me Baby • Sweet Little Angel • Sweet Sixteen • That Evil Child • Three O'clock Blues • The Thrill Is Gone • Troubles, Troubles, Troubles • When My Heart Beats Like A Hammer • A Whole Lot Of Lovin' • The Woman I Love •You're Breaking My Heart • You're Gonna Miss Me.
Catalog No. 07-4030 $19.95

ELMORE JAMES - VITAL BLUES GUITAR - Transcribed by Richard DeVinck
Note-For-Note Tablature transcriptions plus Standard Music Notation. Complete Contents: Can't Stop Lovin' (My Baby) • Canton, Mississippi Breakdown • Dark And Dreary • Dust My Blues • Goodbye Baby • Hawaiian Boogie No. 2 • I Believe • I Held My Baby Last Night • I Was A Fool • Long Tall Woman • Mean And Evil • Sho Nuff I Do • So Mean To Me • Sunnyland • Wild About You Baby.
Catalog No. 07-4029 $19.95

FREDDIE KING - VITAL BLUES GUITAR - Transcribed by Skip Grasso
Note-For-Note Tablature transcriptions plus Standard Music Notation. Another Texas Guitar Great! Photos & bio. None of these songs have ever been in print before !!! Complete contents: Ain't Gonna Worry Anymore • Ain't No Sunshine • Big Legged Woman • Boogie Man • Funky • Hot Tomato • I Wonder Why • I'd Rather Be Blind • Living In the Palace Of The King • My Feeling For The Blues • Play It Cool • Sweet Thing • Wide Open • You Was Wrong.
Catalog No. 07-4040 $19.95

ALBERT COLLINS - VITAL BLUES GUITAR - Transcribed by Richard DeVinck
Note-For-Note Tablature transcriptions plus Standard Music Notation. Includes many great photos & bio. Complete contents: Avalanche • Black Cat Bone • Brick • Ego Trip • Fake I.D. • The Freeze • Ice Pick • Lights Are On But Nobody's Home • Master Charge • Melt Down • The Moon Is Full •Skatin' • Tired Man • Too Tired.
Catalog No. 07-4041 $19.95

LONNIE MACK - VITAL BLUES GUITAR - Transcribed by Richard DeVinck
Note-For-Note Tablature transcriptions plus Standard Music Notation. Never before available. His great songs of his 4 Alligator Albums plus photos and bio. Complete contents: Buffalo Woman • Camp Washington Chili • Cincinnati Jail • Falling Back In Love With You • If You Have To Know • Long Way From Memphis • Me And My Car • The Move •Natural Disaster • Oreo Cookie Blues • Rock And Roll Bones • Satisfy Suzie • A Song I Haven't Sung • Stop • Strike Like Lightning • Tough On Me, Tough On You • Wham! • You Ain't Got Me.
Catalog No. 07-4036 $24.95

CLARENCE "GATEMOUTH" BROWN - VITAL BLUES GUITAR - Transcribed by Skip Grasso
Note-For-Note Tablature transcriptions plus Standard Music Notation. Fantastic guitar pieces from an all-time Texas favorite. Includes bio and photos. Complete contents: Born In Louisiana • Cold Strings • Dollar Got The Blues • Good Looking Woman • I Hate These Doggone Blues • Just Lippin' • Leftover Blues • My Own Prison • Pressure Cooker • Real Life • Sometimes I Slip • Straighten Up •That's Your Daddy Yaddy Yo • What A Shame - What A Shame.
Catalog No. 07-4042 $19.95

If unable to locate, send cover price plus $2.00 per order for shipping to:
Creative Concepts Publishing Corporation